MYSTICISM
IN
NEWBURYPORT

PETER JAMES FORD

BALBOA.
PRESS

A DIVISION OF HAY HOUSE

Balboa Press books may be ordered through booksellers or by contacting:

Balboa Press
A Division of Hay House
1663 Liberty Drive
Bloomington, IN 47403
www.balboapress.com
1 (877) 407-4847

ISBN: 978-1-5043-9184-9 (sc)
ISBN: 978-1-5043-9185-6 (e)

Library of Congress Control Number: 2017918029

Print information available on the last page.

Balboa Press rev. date: 01/12/2018

Contents

In Memory

Louise Hay

(October 8, 1926 - August 30, 2017)

As I learned of Louise's passing, I was deeply saddened. I felt the loss of a great friend and mentor. I, just like so many others, loved this dear, unselfish woman. Not only for all she has done for me through her genuine, sincere and beautiful heart, which is reflected in her books and videos, but she also played a huge part in my personal development and transformation. Through her generosity she provided a way for someone like me (with very limited formal education and with little access to the tools needed to publish a book) to get my book published and promoted on all venues around the world. I owe so much to Louise Hay, Hay House, The Hay House Authors and Balboa Press for the wisdom and guidance to complete this book. Sincere thanks to the people of Balboa Press who supported me and would not let me give up my dream of having my book become a reality. I thank you all with my whole heart, soul and mind. I have been blessed by the presence of Louise Hay in my life, as have so many others.

Sincerely, Peter James Ford

FOREWORD

This will be my first venture into the world of writing. I have no real experience or even any knowledge of how this process works. So, like the first time doing anything, it is sometimes less than perfect. So, if you will, just bear with me as it all unfolds. These were my thoughts as I walked the beach at Long Sands beach in York, Maine, early this morning.

The majority of people in this world unconsciously agree to believe in many conceptions of life that are not even true. They live by manmade rules and misconceptions of life and will defend them violently, if necessary. One of the benefits of thinking for yourself is that you will live in an entirely new and different world than most people are experiencing. It can be Heaven on Earth.

The downside of being awake in this life is that you really can't be yourself with very many of the people that you know. You don't want to be the one, who says the world might not be flat, when the so-called brightest minds of the time believed that the earth being flat was the absolute truth. It was a universally believed misconception that the Earth was flat and it was considered heresy to even question that belief. It is always better to walk softly through this world, as if you were invisible, like a ninja or assassin who comes and goes completely unnoticed.

The purpose of this book is really to give people, from just one more different perspective, an opportunity to think about the possibility that there is more to life and themselves. The reason I am willing to write this book is that the truth can be told in many different ways and each person will respond to different expressions of the same truths, just by being worded a little differently. People's attention will be caught by a simple quote or an unusual way of saying the same information, in just a little different format. Sometimes they respond just because of a personality that they like or from being told by a colorful, mysterious character. There are many different ways that can arouse people's curiosity and it can motivate them to begin their personal search for the truth of their life, once again.

This simple book of tales will be worth all the time and effort if even only one person's heart is touched or just one mind reopens, even for a moment. There is a nut for every bolt and one size does not fit all. So, it is actually a great thing that all these different publications, from all these various authors, are available for all the different types of people in this world.

In regards to the creative power of thought and to the quote, You create your life and your personal world through your thoughts and feelings; I always love to say, What if this was true? Of course, in my life I have lived it for the last twenty-five years, so I have no doubt of its authenticity.

These are some of these eye-opening quotes that I have read over and over and I regard them as priceless inner treasures, much more valuable than gold and silver. With these teachings, you can create all the gold and silver you want, if that is what your heart truly desires. Please take the time and just simply sit quietly and read some of these quotes. Take some time to contemplate them, for even a few moments. To contemplate something is to allow it to dwell in your consciousness, until it reveals its essence to you. Just by allowing something to dwell in your consciousness, it will reveal all it's precious secrets to you. We only need to learn how to just be still and be open to new possibilities. How priceless a gift is that? And how often do most people take the time to do this, even for just a few moments?

In a similar way as contemplation, there is an advanced meditative tool that is called a siddhi. It is using your concentration on a quality or ability that you desire and, through concentration, you can literally draw the desired quality or the ability to yourself and it becomes your own. You can also very easily read people's minds and thoughts. It is not such a great feat, as people's eyes, faces, body language and vibration will reveal to you the story of their lives.

Along the way, on a true spiritual path, you will develop the ability to look right into someone's soul, through the vehicle of his or her eyes. It does not always seem like a gift, as on a number of occasions I would know that their time in their physical body was over, or I sensed a serious illness. The gift of seeing the future also takes a great deal of acceptance of God's will. Well, here are some of these inspirational, life changing, ancient wisdoms that have altered my life.

I ask you, to ask yourself:
"What if the following statements are true?"

Every moment of your life is infinitely creative and the Universe is endlessly bountiful. All you need do is put forth a clear enough request and everything that your heart truly desires must come to you.

(From Creative Visualization,

By Shakti Gawain)

The following words are the trick to creating the necessary feeling to fuel your vision and to magnetically draw it to yourself. This is the quote: "How would you feel, if your deepest desire were already real?" For me, it brings up a strong feeling of happiness and gratitude, that emotion is the fuel and you then direct that feeling/emotion into your visualization and you will literally create your dream from this simple process.

(Ram D. R. Butler,)

Author of Living in the Truth of the Present Moment)

Another secret for coming to believe that your desire is possible, is through the constant, conscious repetition of what it is that you truly want, You come to believe. Barbara, my karmic partner at that time said, that she did not believe she would have the money for some project. I told her that through her willingness to continually, consciously repeat that she already had the money, that this repetition would create the miracle of her believing it to be true, right in her own heart. Then it would be true. And then, it would manifest in the material world. Barbara easily mastered this process.

Consciously repeating the simple phrase of; I am living with all the money I need for this project will cause this thought to go from your conscious mind to being impressed into your subconscious mind, which is a part of the universal mind. Something magical happens from our willingness to consciously repeat the thoughts of our dreams, as if they were 'already real'. Then what happens one day you will all of a sudden say: "Yes, I do believe that it is already real." And then, it is only a matter of time before it manifests in the physical world.

It literally is like God is listening to our thoughts and says, Yes, I will give them that. I cannot repeat enough how important repetition is for success in any endeavor and how well it has worked for me. What does any great athlete or musician do but repeat over and over their practices until they master them. It is also true with anything and everything else.

I have come to learn to love the statements: "It always works, it works every time, with everything and with every one. You can be anything you want and you can have anything you want." What you believe will be true for you, so if you believe this last statement through repetition, it will be true for you. Henry Ford said: "If you believe you can or you believe you can't, you are right." I choose to believe, I am living a charmed life. I am a successful, admired, well-respected, published author.

(Mysticism in Newburyport

By Peter James Ford)

Your feelings are a language that the Universe understands. This intelligent field, which we are a part of, 'responds deeply to human emotion'.

(The Science of Miracles,

By Gregg Braden)

Dr. Carl Jung tells us that the subconscious mind not only contains all of the classified data gathered during all the past lives of the individual, but that it also contains all the wisdom of all the immeasurable ages past. By drawing upon its wisdom and power, the individual may possess the good things of life in great abundance.

(Quote taken from, Key to Yourself,

By Carl Jung)

You remember the story of Aladdin's lamp? The lamp represents the conscious mind and the rubbing of the lamp means understanding. The genie represents the subconscious mind, that mighty power within yourself awaiting for recognition and unfoldment, that when aroused and used will bring you to the realization of your fondest dreams.

(From, Key to Yourself,

By Venice Bloodworth)

In the entire Universe there can be no such thing as luck or fate; every action, every thought, is governed by law. Behind every bit of good fortune lies the cause that we ourselves have sometime, somewhere set in motion. Behind all ill fortune we will find the energy we, ourselves, have generated. Every cause, (which is our thoughts) must have a certain definite effect; there is no dodging the results. We reap what we sow with 'exact mathematical precision'.

(From, Key to Yourself

By Venice Bloodworth)

Every thought is a prayer.

(Unity Church)

There is 'no such thing', as an idle thought.

(From, What's on my mind?

By Swami Anantanada)

People don't have *the time* to do things right the first time, but they always have *the time* to do it over again.

(Owner of the Monster Chopper called *Blood Lust*)

You need not leave your room. Remain sitting at your table and listen. You need not even listen, simply wait, you need not even wait, just learn to become quiet and still and solitary. The world will freely offer itself to you to be unmasked, it has no choice; it will roll in ecstasy at your feet.

(Quote By, Franz Kafka)

The intelligence behind Nature, which is God, is in 'every cell of our body', giving us direct access to the powers of God, through how we use our thinking processes, which is the cause of every detail in every moment.

Radiant, Golden White Light is the greatest healer in this entire Universe. Radiant Golden White Light brings healing to wherever it is directed. Visualize breathing in this Golden White light into every cell in your body and repeat: "I am in perfect health. I am 100 percent healed." See and feel this Radiant Golden White Light flowing into every cell of your body and this regular practice will give you perfect health.

(Ram D. R. Butler,

Author of Living in the Truth of the Present Moment)

We are riding the back of a giant (Consciousness/God) and all we need do is learn how 'to whisper in its ear'. We learn how to whisper in God's ear by going into the silence then going to that place between thoughts and we release our desire, that is the equivalent of whispering in the ear of the giant.

(From, an Internet Program,

by Dr. Joe Dispenza)

You are the designer of your destiny. You are the author. You write the story. The pen is in your hand and the outcome is whatever you choose.

(From the Secret,

by Lisa Nichols)

There is no blackboard in the sky on which God has written your purpose, your mission in life. The blackboard does not exist, so your purpose is what you say it is. Your mission is the mission you give yourself. Your life will be what you create it as and no one will stand in judgment of it now or ever.

(From the Secret,

By Neale Donald Walsch)

Our body is the product of our thoughts. Science has found that thoughts and emotions actually determine the physical substance and structure and function of our bodies.

(From the Secret,

By Dr. John Hagelin)

Science (quantum physicists) have proven what the ancient spiritual masters have always known. It is a proven scientific fact now that our thoughts and feelings converging in our heart as an emotion actually affects our CELLS, can even change our DNA and the ATOMS in our bodies and the world around us. That changes all the beliefs that physics was based on and it is a new day for everyone.

(Science of Miracles,

By Gregg Braden)

There is but one power, one force in this entire Universe and we control it through how we direct our thoughts.

(Ram D. R. Butler

Author of Living in the Truth of the Present Moment)

A boxer will train throwing punches and combinations, over and over and they will become impressed in his subconscious mind and he will react to a situation without even thinking about it consciously. Because the constant repetition, whether throwing punches or kicks or repeating positive thoughts, will go from the conscious mind to the subconscious mind and also to the unconscious mind (which is the physical body) and actually, from this repetition, *the mind is now in the body.* The body (unconscious mind) will do things automatically that have been repeated over and over, whether through physical acts or your thoughts and feelings.

I have been repeating few affirmations so often that now I will hear them coming from inside me, similar to when you can't get a song out of your head. And they are releasing healing chemicals all the time. These few affirmations are as follows: "Everything is all right, there is nothing wrong and there actually, was never anything wrong." And "Everything goes my way." "Everything has worked itself out, even better, than I could have ever imagined."

With every thought, there is a chemical release. The negative fearful thoughts release the stress hormone cortisone and scientists have proven that the stress from this continued release will deplete the immune system and this is the source of all illnesses. And once again, the problems go back to the original cause and that is your thoughts. So if you are repeating positive thoughts, you are releasing healing chemicals, including cancer-fighting chemicals, in your body and you can actually heal yourself from any and all illnesses.

The work that Gregg Braden and Dr. Joe Dispenza are doing has taken it to new unlimited levels of healing. Any and all types of illnesses, including so-called incurables, are being reversed. Actually, the word incurable means curable from within.

I can never repeat it enough, that if you want health or success in life you need to understand your own mind and control your thoughts. "It is all about the mind." When you can see that it is the universal energy that does everything and not us, you will experience a new world. The Universe not only does everything, it does everything "with Zero effort." All, your struggling and trying to control things is just a total waste of your precious time and energy. If you truly want something, the way to do it is to see it and feel it, like it is already real. Our work is convincing ourselves that it is already real; this is done through continued repetition.

The secret is creating the happy and grateful feeling of it already existing, by thinking to yourself, "how would I feel if this was already true." What that does for me is creates a feeling of happiness and gratitude. Once you touch upon that feeling, you direct it into your visualization and your dream is already created. It will be "compelled to manifest" in the physical world.

That is the formula for creating whatever you want. Once you master this process, you will be the Master of Your Life. The way a child thinks, so innocently, about what they want at Christmas, is the marvelous gift of imagination. We all have this gift of imagination and it is the simple creative tool, to bring anything into existence.

(Peter's beliefs)

Imagination is everything. It is the preview of life's coming attractions.

(Albert Einstein)

You create your own Universe as you go along.

(Winston Churchill)

See yourself living in abundance and you will attract it. It always works; it works every time, with every person.

If you see it in your mind, you're going to hold it in your hand.

(From the Secret,

By Bob Proctor)

You could start with nothing and out of nothing and out of no way, *a way would be made.*

Whatever thoughts have done in your life, *it can be undone,* through a shift in your awareness. The moment you begin to think properly, there is something that is within you, there is power in you that's greater than the world. It will begin to emerge. It will take over your life, it will clothe you, it will guide you, protect you. Direct you. Sustain your very existence, *if you will let it.*

(From the Secret,

By Michael Beckwith D.D. Visionary)

Put your whole heart, soul and mind into even the smallest act and this is the secret to success. God gives us everything we want and as far as God's concerned, "what we think, is what we want." Then God gives us what we have been thinking. We carry within us, the most powerful creative device in the entire Universe: It is the Mind, of the human individual, we might think of the mind as a small thing, yet, Infinite Energy fuels it.

(Ram D. R. Butler

Author of Living in the Truth of the Present Moment)

The following is so important to know. When you first wake in the morning and just before you go to sleep, are the two times that you can most influence your mind. First thing in the morning, put your attention on your intentions and they will influence your entire day. Most of the day you are running on automatic and you can consciously set your mind in the direction you want by focusing, first thing in the morning. What you think just before going to sleep will play over and over in your subconscious mind for the duration of your night's sleep. While you sleep is a powerful time to create your desires and we do this by focusing our thoughts on what we want, just as we are falling into sleep. The subconscious mind will do the rest.

(Dauchsy Meditations)

Learn to recognize and listen to your intuition, which is your sixth sense. It is truly God talking to you. God wants to give us a win in every situation and all we have to do is to learn to listen to this inner guidance. One of the most valuable things that I have learnt is how to listen to my intuition, which is God and our sixth sense and how to cultivate this ability and to use it in every moment.

Also, which is huge, is recognizing the power of gratitude. God will bestow even more gifts and blessings to the individual that is grateful for what he has right now. Gratitude attracts to you more things to be grateful for. Like attracts like.

My morning prayer is one of gratitude for all God has given me and for all that God has done for me. I thank God with my whole heart for always having filled all my needs, wants and even all my desires. I thank God for always having kept me safe and fully protected, especially from myself and my self-destructive tendencies. I willing do my part with thinking less and when I do think, of having only kind, positive, uplifting thoughts on my mind. I do my part by being kind and helpful to whoever enters my karmic sphere. But, I leave my life and myself unconditionally in God's hands. I make a daily decision to go all the way and turn my life and will over to the care of the God of my understanding. This God has always made my heart beat, even in the womb, and gives me the gift of life through its breath in every moment. My wildest desires pale compared to what God has planned for me. I abandon myself completely to this unconditional loving presence. I ask in the morning: "What do you have in mind for me?" and I know it will be the gifts of the most loving father you could imagine. I am open to the even better new life God has in mind for me. Thank you God with my whole heart and being.

(Peter James Ford)

Anger is a very powerful emotion. Your anger can make you feel like a bulletproof, steroidal superman. What you don't see is the angry man a few days later when he comes down from this burst of this dangerous emotion because he will be exhausted and hiding under the covers. That is how it was for me. The hate is like racing fuel, which makes the hot rod go really fast, but burns up the engine. Hate and anger are two of the worse things for your health. That baseball bat that you want to use on your enemies, you actually are using it on yourself. Your brain can't tell the difference between you and another and gives you first, whatever you are wishing for someone else.
Hate destroys the Hater.

(Peter James Ford)

We must be willing to get rid of the life we've planned, so as to have the life that is waiting for us. Follow your bliss and the Universe will open doors for you where there were only walls.

The goal of life is to make your heartbeat match the beat of the Universe, to match your nature with Nature.

(Just some of the wisdom,

by Joseph Campbell)

The day that I saw clearly how God is like the most unselfish, unconditional loving father that I could possibly ever have changed my life forever. All God wants to do is love me and give me a win in every situation, in every moment. God is so unselfish that God shares all of its powers with me and holds nothing back for itself. How could I ever worry about anything ever again? Where is there to go, what is there to do, when you are already in the presence of God? When I experienced this eternal truth, I found the love and acceptance that I had always longed for. This love brought me complete contentment. God's love resides right within my own heart and the 'only destination' is my own heart. Don't waste your time looking anywhere else.

(Peter James Ford)

I am perfectly healthy, strong, young and full of life, powerful, loving; harmonious, successful in life, successful at living, happy, money is no longer a concern. When you repeat positive affirmations about yourself you impress your subconscious mind with just those qualities as a basis for the new character you are building. This character will attract to itself conditions that correspond to it in kind and quality; you remember that the subconscious mind does not argue or prove, but only goes to work and brings about conditions that the conscious mind believes to be true. The conscious repetition of what you want is the secret method to bring you to believe your desire is true. If you believe it, it is so. So the work is convincing ourselves that it is already real (through conscious repetition) and then the Universe will take care of the details.

(From, Key to Yourself

By Venice Bloodworth)

When you change the way you look at things, the things you look at will change.

(Wayne Dyer)

The intelligence that made the body can heal the body.

(Dr. Joe Dispenza)

The things we loved and lost are 'worthy' of our grief. So, let yourself feel what you feel.

(Cheryl Richardson, Hay House Author)

These are a few of the beliefs that have changed my life, through the continual, conscious repetition of them. They are the absolute truth for me and they make my time here a completely enjoyable ride through God's country. I hope you take some time and contemplate them and see for yourself.

I love to ask people, "But what if these statements are true?" I realized along the way that a few words at just the right time could reawaken an individual to their true identity. A great example is my friend Ritchie, who just prior to dying of multiple gunshot wounds in 1968 had mentioned a book he was reading. He talked of how the book mentioned being in a powerful river and going with the flow. After a day and night of drinking and drugging, I literally sobered up, only for a few moments, but it was long enough to reawaken memories of past spiritual practices. I did remember and knew this was not my first rodeo. My hope is to pass on this gift and if I have to reveal all my secrets (well most of them) to help even one person remember their true purpose, it will be worth it.

One day as I was driving along and thinking negative thoughts about a relationship that I was involved in; I thought these next few words. These words have proven to be one of the most powerful tools I have ever come across and they just came out of the blue. The simple phrase was: "Don't I have anything better than this to have on my mind?" I knew instantly that I had a choice about what I thought about next and anything, even a simple thought of walking the beach, was something much better than what I had on my mind in that moment. Remember that there is a chemical release in your body with every thought. Stress thoughts release cortisol, which eventually will deplete your immune system and be the cause of all your illnesses. Positive, uplifting, loving, kind, forgiving thoughts will actually release chemicals that will rejuvenate your health and even prevent cancer. So, which thoughts sound better to you?

These are just a few of the life-changing words that have helped me. I could fill a dozen books with the notes I have acquired so far and maybe that will be a future book, from my seventy notebooks. Hope you enjoy this book of lighthearted tales from just another seeker whose heart is overflowing with love and gratitude for this life that God has given me.

Below is a picture of Thunderhaven and our Bikes;
Thunderhaven was the country home that Barb and I created.

From one of the most grateful people you will ever met, wishing
you a "Safe Ride" on your personal journey.
Sincere Thanks to All
Peter James Ford

"DEDICATION"

This book of lighthearted tales is Dedicated To Rachel Elizabeth Ford
&
Shayla Elizabeth Howell

Shayla deep in thought. Is this character really my Grandpa?

Through the excellent parenting of my wonderful and gifted daughter Rachel, this young girl Shayla has flourished and become a perfectly healthy, extremely capable, highly intelligent, young, wonderful girl. Shayla has been a blessing for our entire family and I have witnessed Shayla, like Rachel, both come into this world in a highly evolved state, as very creative individuals.

Rachel knew exactly how to allow Shayla, through unconditional love, to express her creative abilities without suppressing her or her gifts. I have watched with great respect and admiration as my daughter Rachel, the best mother ever, skillfully give Shayla the breathing room to express her divinity, while at the same time keeping her safe and fully cared for by being a completely devoted, loving parent. Shayla's companionship has been such a gift for me and she touches everyone's heart she meets.

Shayla in the Wind

One day when Shayla was five years old, she turned and said to me, "I came into this world to bring love." She truly has done that with many people around her already. She has melted my heart. Shayla, even at her young age, loved Grandpa's 'show and go' custom motorcycles and would climb right up on them, so naturally, and pose for pictures for our yearly motorcycle calendars. We made calendars every year, for the past ten years, of our trips to the White Mountains and of our friends and fellow riders.

"I Look Gooood!"

Shayla riding Pete's Dragon. Dragon was one of my motorcycles that she especially loved, a Thunder Mountain Keystone, and when I sold it she was furious with me. She still looks at me with a very serious, disapproving frown, any time it is mentioned. I think Shayla felt it was her bike. It is kind of humorous that the interactions between males and females, whatever their ages are, always seemed so similar. They say, on a spiritual level, that age means nothing and that's why an adult can share something special with even a young baby. It is just so humorous to have this interaction with this little innocent person. She just reaches in and touches my heart so gently. One day, I told Shayla we would build a special motorcycle for her and she said: "I want flames coming over the tank and animals painted all over the bike." I said: "This would be an expensive bike, but don't worry about the cost because I will take care of everything." She smiled and cocked her head and said, "I'm a kid. I never worry about money." What a gift that is, the innocence of a child and if we are lucky enough our paths will return us back to the place we started from and live in peace and total freedom with the innocence of a child.

Remember when you were a child on those days that you stood on the beach, feeling the radiant sun warm your face and a gentle sea breeze glide across your skin and felt the sand on your bare feet, between your toes and then listened to the sounds of the ocean with 'nothing on your mind'. That is truly being in the presence of God. That is the time you are truly in the Truth of the Present Moment. Please take time to re-experience those moments, before this temporary illusion of a physical life is over.

Shayla has been in the Christmas play in the York school system every year and when the performance would end, they would first allow all the children to run down the aisle to their families. Well, last year Shayla ran over to me and yelled "Grandpa" and her words were so full of love and happiness. It truly was the happiest moment of my life. She was so happy that I had come to her play and that I was there for her. I was the lucky one. I experienced overwhelming 'Unconditional Love' in that moment. There have been a number of times when the day was done and Shayla and I were sitting quietly and the world had slowed down, when the little girl would disappear and this little, old soul would show up and quietly ask a deep philosophical question about life or reincarnation. This silly Irishman would also disappear and be replaced with a clear channel for God to talk with this little one, who is truly a manifestation of God. An incredible conversation would transpire. I would truly feel the presence of God, of Pure Consciousness, and felt that my whole life had led up to this moment to be a messenger, a clear channel for her. All my work and pain was all worth it to be able to be here for her. In a way I feel that it is my way of making up for a loveless life.

I felt that God was using me as a vehicle to let this information flow back to her, when in reality all that was happening was that she was remembering what she already knew. Carl Yung says that the subconscious mind not only knows all of this past life but all of our past lives; and not only that, but our subconscious mind knows all the immeasurable knowledge that has ever been known to anyone over the ages.

I knew the other night that I had gone to the same source, the subconscious mind, that is part of universal mind, that others have gone to and became successful writers. So how could I not also be completely successful? This is available to all of us through our subconscious mind, which is the source of all knowledge and all power for the individual.

They say that we are only using five or ten % of our brain/mind power. Seems like that is the conscious mind's limit, but through the practice of meditation and silence we can tap into our subconscious mind which is the other ninety percent, actually unlimited, and be directly connected to the universal mind. The Universal mind is the source of all knowledge and power.

I would laugh after Shayla and I would have our deep exchanges, in the quiet of the night. I said: "Someday you will remember our late night conversations when the world was still asleep and think I have the coolest grandpa." She did not comment but she just quietly gave me that look she has when she is mulling something over. I watch her eyes, as she processes stuff. I can see the wheels turning and it is really validating everything I have been learning in my readings. Shayla has been one of my great teachers.

It is such a pleasure to see her express herself without all the self-consciousness that we develop along the way. I had shown her a picture of my brother Phil, she smiled and said, "Yeah, I know him, that's The Pirate." I had to agree that Phil would fit right in with the Pirates of the Caribbean.

Brother Phil

I have learned so much from her. When she was very young and just becoming aware of things, her mother said: "Shayla, this is your Grandpa." I watched as she looked at my eyes and face and I could see her actually forming the conception of, "Oh, this is a Grandpa." It was an amazing experience for me to see the look of awareness in her eyes, as a conception of life was being formed. It is burnt into my memory.

Grandpa and Shayla
"Look at the conscious awareness in her eyes, just amazing."

If we are aware in the present moment, then all the secrets of life are right there for us to be completely revealed. That's why it is so important to take time to be still, just be quiet, as all the work is done in the silence. One day when we were working in the back woods on our property, we took a break and sat down. We loved working on the Cider hill property. Barbara, my significant other, would always have peanut butter crackers for Shayla that she loved.

While we were sitting quiet she shared that someone had been mean to her. I had asked her to always tell her mother or me if anyone was ever unkind to her and she had promised. I felt this gentle, innocent child confide in me and trusted me enough to share her hurt feelings. I was so touched by her gentleness. Once again, I felt that my whole life had been to finally arrive at this place, for her. There truly is a worthwhile purpose for me in this present moment.

One of my regrets in this life is that I did not have the emotional ability or understanding to be able to be there for my children in the way I can be here for Shayla now. I know it sounds a little like one of those individuals who sees the light (hallelujah!) and then the things of the material world become meaningless to them. But it just seemed so obvious that all the outside worldly stuff is pretty unfulfilling and it is all about what we share. The singer B.J. Thomas, after having had a spiritual awakening said, "All we have is what we share." D. R. Butler (Ram) writes about this, in the beginning of his Course of Training called "Living in the Truth of the Present Moment." He writes that we can see it now or we can wait and eventually see it later but that "life is all about service." My close friend Big Ben, a lifelong legendary Biker, who was in the movie about the story of the number one riding club, had gotten born again and after his awakening Ben spent his life in service. Ben would also say, the same truth about a life of service. Ben, like Ram, was someone who truly walked the talk, regarding this simple principle.

In Memory of Richard "Big Ben" Benedict

This picture was taken of Cathy, Big Ben, at one of my weddings with me on the left. Ben left us with these words: "Until we meet again." I thought that a life of service was not for me until recently. I have always spent my life trying to get my share and even more than my share. I had the more, more, more thing. It is interesting that when you are living a life of giving, you actually never have to worry about receiving. You will get whatever you are giving out. These are the times that someone shows true courage when you go against all your preconceived ideas of how things should be and be true to yourself, despite what all the ones around you are saying.

Well, the day came, after awakening to the realization that there was more to life and that I had already gotten my share and more and that now I could finally think of someone else. If it can happen to a selfish old pirate like myself then miracles really can happen. I have lived a pretty self-centered life and have not done a great job at being there for other people in the past. And, I was considered by some to be a mean and dangerous person. So, to have this gentle, old soul (Shayla) trust me enough to confide in me, well, it just melted my heart. My heart was as closed and hard as a rock most of my life but over the years, through grace, it has burst wide opened. This is another reason for my sincere appreciation of my re-awakening in this life.

I am also grateful for the gift of knowing that God dwells within me as me. I am grateful for the personal development that spontaneously follows the opening of a human heart. It may seem silly to most but it made me feel that my life has not been a waste and has given me purpose to be there for Shayla, Rachel and my son Benjamin in whatever ways I can. When I shared my thoughts of my granddaughter with Kay Butler, the wife of D. R. Butler, she said, "Shayla is obviously an old soul who has come into your life to help you." I could not agree more and I am so grateful for the love I experience with her. Ram's course has been a priceless gift and has been my daily companion for twenty-five years. Similar to Carl Yung's experience after reading *The Tibetan book of the Dead*, which became his daily constant companion. It is interesting that the book called *The Tibetan Book of the Dead* was the book that triggered my re-awakening in this lifetime.

Shayla's unconditional love showed me that I was more than I believed I was and that I have real purpose with whatever time I have left in this body. My experiences with Shayla showed me that I could be a channel or messenger for God. What an honor to be God's messenger. The past is gone and all we have is this moment, so for me to have purpose in this moment gives me a feeling it has all been worth it. My purpose will probably be only for the rare few that I am meant to play a part for. Only the present moment is real, as I experienced through the Course of Training "Living in The Truth of The Present Moment." My next thought is, so *that means, nothing else exists from the past, 'if it even existed back then'.* My perceptions of what went on probably were not even very accurate or maybe not even true. It made it easy to forget the past. Let it go and move on to this new day. Thanks Ram, once again, for this priceless information.

Early one morning, I was sitting in meditation and I heard Shayla come down the stairs. She climbed into her special chair with her blanket and sat there very quietly. After a while she said: "I am going to use my mind to bring the meditation bell in the living room back into this room. Don't open your eyes." I tried to contain my laughter and felt this feeling of joy as I heard her sneak into the other room and grab our meditation bell and then very stealthily climb back into her chair, like a little Ninja. She rang the bell three times and said: "I never left the chair and I only used my mind to bring the bell to me." We both then laughed for the longest time. What are the chances that I would get to share time with someone who shares my same loves and has the same sense of humor? I truly have been blessed.

When D. R. Butler (Ram) started his new course it was at the same time that Shayla was born and also Kay and Ram's grandchild was born, seven years now. And seven has been such a reoccurring, significant number in my life, just kind of interesting, how things coincide. Deepak Chopra talks about his young grandchild and is in awe of the wisdom that this child possesses. Many elders and wise ones have said that at this time many highly evolved beings (who lived and died many years ago in places like Egypt, India and Tibet) are being reincarnated to this world to help us in these trying times. They say it explains how these young children are so proficient at computers, math and the sciences. It certainly would explain the fast-paced changes in technology. That is what helped me accept the past life thing. People could not learn all that they know in just one lifetime; it is obvious that it has taken many, many lifetimes for people to be where they are, with this accumulated knowledge.

I asked Shayla what she wanted to be when she grew up. She said: "I thought I wanted to be a veterinarian." She then said: "That was before my singing voice came in." She continued: "My singing voice did not come in until I was five and then I knew I was going to be a famous singer." Shayla then said: "Besides, I will already be known worldwide and famous because of our book." The proper self-esteem and healthy confidence this girl has amazes me. Rachel has truly broken the chain of unhealthy attitudes that have been passed down through our family for eons; with the way she has raised Shayla.

Shayla and I have been taking many walks on the beach with my great friend Tyler and his beloved dog Penny and his absolutely beautiful girlfriend Dana (tall, long legged, dark-haired beauty). Along with us comes Dana's dog Griffin, a rescue dog named after the mythological creature made up of a lion and an eagle. The dog lovers' special place is Long Sands Beach, in Maine with many, many rescue dogs. Which says a lot about the hearts of the people of Maine. Shayla is in heaven there, as she loves the animals. As I watch her living and loving fearlessly, compassionately and full of unconditional love, I know she will be a natural healer and she actually already is one.

So, to the little soul (Shayla), I dedicate my book.
Love Grandpa

Shayla riding the 120 Race

SINCERE THANKS TO ONE AND ALL

I was sitting quietly, in meditation, at the beach house in York Harbor, Maine, on a wintry Wednesday night. I was nice and warm and all safe and secure. I was to hear a couple, man and woman, outside on the street arguing. It is dark, cold and they appeared intoxicated and also sounded very unhappy. And for whatever reason, they were also on foot. I was grateful that the man seemed to control his anger and did not physically hurt her, as I would have had to leave the peace of my evening meditation and stop him. I felt empathy for their personal struggle, as it was a cold night to be out in that kind of situation.

Today, it seems so senseless, all the conflict and struggle that goes on in people's lives. It is basically blaming others for the life 'you have created for yourself' or past karma that you have to experience. Most of my life has also been consumed with the same struggle and strife of fighting people, places and things, when all the time I was just fighting myself.

As I sat there, I remembered a night from my past of being drunk and in a blackout. (A blackout is a drunken state, where you do not remember anything.) As I recall, that particular night from my past I remembered regaining consciousness as I was running in the woods. I was cold and covered with blood, not knowing whose blood it was, mine or someone else's, and hearing sirens in the distance. I can remember the physical sick feeling in my belly and the feeling of what I call 'soul sickness', as clearly as if it was happening right now.

In this section, I will try to stay focused on giving thanks and recognition to all the individuals, including supportive people, groups, so called gang members, people labeled criminals, family, friends, ashrams, a 12-step program, spiritual centers, sages and saints, hoodlums and bad asses, including training gyms, training brothers, etc., that God has worked through to play their part for me in this incarnation.

I would have to start this list by mentioning having the best parents possible for me. I just spent St. Patrick's Day in the White Mountains. My father, being a good Irishman, died on St. Patty's Day a few years ago. I feel his presence more than ever, as if he were right here, right now, which he is. No one really dies; it is only the temporary physical body that falls away. 'Our true essence is of an eternal nature'. No one really goes anywhere, as the physical and spiritual worlds are intertwined. These worlds, the physical world and the so-called afterlife, are right here, right now, fully immersed with each other. You cannot separate them. Also, the past, the present and the future are all fully available right now, in consciousness. In consciousness there is no time. I thank both my parents for having put up with such a troubled child. My father once said that I was a tortured soul. There was a lot of truth in that statement.

Also, at the very top of this list are Louise Hay and Hay House International Publishing House and Balboa Press for providing such a generous and unselfish avenue for people like myself to tell their stories unimpeded, and to be published and made available internationally.

The White Mountain National Forest was a place my father and mother would take my three brothers and myself camping and hiking when we were kids. Those are some of the fondest memories I have. Sunny days feeling the warm sun on my face, smelling the unique scent of the pine trees, breathing truly clean, fresh air and swimming in the pure, pristine, but freezing cold streams and rivers flowing down from the mountains from the past winter's snow. It truly was a time of innocence, of just being in nature. It was really my first experience of 'simply being', which I was to know later as a way of life. At that time in my life being in the mountains or being at the beach was the only momentary peace I knew. I spent a childhood of endless mental anguish and restlessness, until I had my first drink of the magic elixir, alcohol. I treasure my 'Peace of Mind' and feel it is one of the greatest gifts I have today. Soon, I will be back up in the sunny mountains in the spring air, riding my Harley Road Bike and sharing the day with Sandi, my sidekick.

Peter on early spring run to the mountains with snow capped Mt. Washington in the background. Sincere Thanks to my parents, for this wonderful gift of exposing me to Nature. We would leave the Mountains and would return to our home in Lynn, Mass, on a Sunday night. As, we would enter into Sin City; a sense of impending doom, a black cloud, and a fearful depression would just consume me. We were back in the badlands. Well, I have returned to these mountains and have spent many, many incredible years riding motorcycles up there. How lucky I am, to have these White Mountains to ride in and to have the best of the bikes, built by Harley Davidson and Thunder Mountain Custom Cycle. I feel like the mountains are my home and it is just a quick two-hour ride up from York Harbor, Maine, on my custom Harley that the racing techs of Seacoast Harley Davidson have built specifically for me. I have sincere thanks to the whole team. Well, who would not be grateful to be riding along the seacoast of NH and Maine and then spending time in the Mountains? Then followed by riding down in the Florida Sun, or out in the high desert area of New Mexico and Arizona. I truly am glad I have lived long enough to experience this other world.

The Ford Brothers: Peter, Skip, Phil, and Paul

Ford Brothers 1990's

Brother Phil
"In the Wind"

My Cousins Rick and Tom, Brother Phil and myself at Seacoast Harley, shortly before Tom's passing.

In Memory
Cousin Tom

Little River Inn, Lynn ~ Mass.

Family, Friends, Brothers and Riders of Sin City

I will continue this gratitude list by mentioning my son Benjamin, my daughter Rachel and my granddaughter Shayla.

I would like to give special thanks to Barbara Eleanor Parton who taught me so much about life and showed how I could have so much more. I was privileged to share ten incredible years with her. Barbara not only freely shared herself with me, including her gift of physical beauty, but also her numerous homes in the US and Mexico, her possessions, and her wealth. Barb was not only a best friend and a great lover, but also a true mentor, who by her example showed me there are no limits to my greatness, including worldly wealth. Barb not only gave me the experience of living in financial wealth but also showed me that I could easily create my own financial abundance, if that was what my heart truly desired. They say that monetary wealth, money, is one of the most 'malleable' of all substances; for me that meant easily attainable, or easily changed or created.

Barb was someone who had done it all, second in her engineering class at Cal Poly, consultant for Fortune Five Hundred companies around the world, including Harley dealerships. She had acquired worldly riches while always studying spiritual principles. Having Barbara, as an example, and having the principles of truth to guide me, worldly success has also become my reality today. Today I have wealth in all areas of life, including worldly wealth. Our time together, our karma, has been completed and I had to accept that I had to share her and her love with others in the world, as she was meant to play her part for them. Yes, it took some time to accept this change, but I knew she was very, very happy being out in California, doing her thing of helping people. Her happiness is the most important thing for me. I truly wish her the best. I knew her heart was in California and she is truly a California kind of girl.

The picture below is of Barbara and me on one of our many trips to the White Mountains. Barbara is truly one beautiful woman and she can really handle the big bikes. Her riding days began out in California, many years ago.

"Best Wishes to Barbara"

I love the following statement: "If I accept and respect the world 'as it is' the world will accept and respect me, as I am." This means that if I adopt this attitude I will get back the same respect and acceptance that I give and be able to live my life in peace and in a lifestyle of my choosing. I love choices and the freedom and power that go with them. There is something magical about writing stuff out. And this simple process is paying me huge dividends with a deeper acceptance and appreciation of the changes that have occurred in my life. That is the miracle of the 12-step program and spiritual work that a self-consumed man like myself could be capable of experiencing unconditional love today.

These writings have made me aware of how abundantly blessed I have been in love and friendship. I have had the privilege of being with more than my share of wonderful women and have had countless great friend from all walks of life, from Yale to Jail. The people that have been in my life are a priceless gift. Dave Nock said to me, regarding our friendship, that it was something you could not buy with money. I agree. I was to see numerous examples of this kind of friendship at the Hard Nock's Gym. It was a place where I saw what I would call 'a true brotherhood'.

Today I look at the ending of this relationship with Barbara as if one of us had died and, instead of being sad, 'being grateful for the time that we shared together'. Everything in this world is so very temporary and one day it will all disappear. It is such a valuable lesson to learn how to let go and not hold on to anything in this life too tightly, 'including life itself'.

Some of us may help one or two people in our lifetime but people like Barb, Ram and Kay are ones who will help many. Barbara was given a very fitting name from a group she participated in: "Loving Light." I owe her a lot and she will always have a special place in my heart. I am sure we have been together in past lives and will play parts for each other in future ones. The end of Barbara's and my time together has been the catalyst that motivated me to complete this book of tales that has sat unfinished for seven years. So, she really deserves the credit for the completion of this book of lighthearted tales.

A friend once told me that when we are young we think we will only love one person in this life, but that actually there could be many we love over the course of our lifetime. Surprisingly enough, it has turned out true for me; today there are a number of wonderful women that have a precious piece, of my heart.

Great thanks to D. R. Butler (Ram), author of "Living in the Truth of the Present Moment" and Kay Butler, his wife, who have been such a blessing on my journey. Ram and Kay are remarkable examples of selfless service. They are just, truly nice, kind, gentle, generous, loving, highly evolved individuals. I must say the most singularly influencing spiritual material in my life has been the daily readings of Ram's course on the principles of truth. I have studied and practiced these teachings for the past twenty-five years. Their Course of Training is about living in the truth of the present moment and deserves the majority of credit for any wisdom that may be found in these tales. My thanks go to Ram and Kay and the course.

If you enjoy 'the energy' in these stories I would highly recommend investigating Ram's course, as it is really the source of my connection with the eternal truths coming from a lineage of true Masters. The worldwide community of participants of Ram's course has been the only place I truly ever fit. I was too good for the bad and too bad for the good. But I found my place, my fellowship with the course participants. Also, I have found an acceptance of who I am within the teachings of this course. I thank the meditation Master of this Yogic path I followed, for having 'energized' and brought the 'actual experience' of these ancient teachings into my life and for his being the vehicle that has created this book. I truly believe it really is his book. To, the present spiritual leader for allowing me the experience of meeting her and knowing I was in the presence of a living meditation Master. When I looked into her eyes all I saw was 'pure consciousness', a pure, thought-free mind. I literally was looking into a mirror and then this living Master disappeared and this presence of consciousness was all that was left. Which I just can't describe in words. I heard her voice in my mind say without words: "Is there anything else that you need?" My reply was No, as I felt so intoxicated that I could barely walk away. And that was from just being near her. The experience of meeting someone at that level of development was another of the greatest gifts I have received on my journey.

I thank all the folk from the 12-step program, to Tim, my sponsor in my beginning years. And I also thank Tim's sponsor, Jack B., a colorful figure from the early beginning days of the New York 12-step program. Jack had also been studying some type of Eastern philosophy where he lived in upper New York State. Through these sponsors, I was hearing about these ancient principles of truth, even in my early days in the program. This program, along with grace, has given me sobriety since March of 1970.

Everyone from the spiritual retreat centers, the meditation Masters, the Swamis and monks from the centers who I had many, many wonderful late night talks with, friends from the centers, Faith, Katherine, Eleanor and Martha, for being so helpful and supportive in regard to my writings. Shipley, the minister of Unity on the River, the great bookstore staff of Unity, Denise, Robin and all the loving people from Unity.

This in many ways was the hardest piece to write, as there have been so many great people that God has worked through to help me and literally save my life on a number of occasions. Some of the others from the Newburyport area are, Trish, Jeff, Dave B., Maureen, Joe, Frank, Karen, Cathy A. and Al. As I have said: "I may have omitted many, but you all have my gratitude for having played your part in my life."

My Great Friend, Matt

To Richie, who back in the sixties was the messenger to help reawaken me in this life regarding spiritual practices from past lives. Some of the others from this area around Newburyport are; Jack, Cliff B., Michelle, a magnificent, tall, dark haired beauty, Boss Barry.

BOSS BARRY

To the members of the riding club from the Lynn area who saved my life on more than one occasion. Tyler, Dana, Bruce, Gay, all my friends from Gold's Gym, The Nock Family and the gang from Hard Nock's Gym, the most stand-up crew you ever could meet. To John Cena and his brothers, Alyssa White Feather for her unconditional gift of opening my heart. To Layne, The Mystery Woman of Newburyport, Dick Sewell, Teamster Boss and his family, brothers from the truckers union and associates from the union 'Goon Squad' from the sixties and seventies. Thanks to the Wise Guys that I met through the Boston unions, who turned out to be powerful friends. Ellen M., a little sweetheart that I shared three of the most wonderful years with. Bobby Joe, Nadine, a young absolutely beautiful, amazingly talented woman, who healed me after my first divorce. That might be my next book, *The women that healed me after my divorces*. Sandi M., Andy, Kristy, another magnificent dark-haired woman who played on the US Olympic Team,

'Newburyport Phil'

RIDER

In Memory,
Brother, Pat
9 /3/ 11

Art H., a great lifelong friend, John N., Big Mike R., Tommy H., Karen, an absolutely gorgeous woman who gave me the incredible gift of the book called *Key to Yourself*, Andy, Kenny B., Earl B., friends from the Wilton center, friends from the Boston center, friends from the Miami and Sarasota centers. Jen, a breathtakingly beautiful, loving, kind and gifted woman, Robert C., the Dragonfly Inn gang, Stu, Sumner, Jeff, John, Colin and Joanna, Norman-mountain man, a generous great friend, Bob H., All of the Fahey family. Beth Fahey, a sweetheart of a woman who will always have a special place in my heart. Beth is the owner of the "Brick House Fitness."

Special Thanks
To my riding buddies
from Quebec

One summer day Barbara and I were at Bentley Warren's Saloon in Arundel, Maine when these two cutie pies rolled into the Saloon's camping grounds on full size Harleys from Quebec. I told Barbara that we had to take a photo of them for our collection of pictures hanging in the garages. The girls were happy to join in the photo shoot and when they finished, they were heading back to the campgrounds. One of the sweethearts looked at me and with a very sexy French accent said, "Time for a showerrrrr." I looked to Barbara and said, "If I am included in this showerrrrr, you have to cut me some slack about this whole marriage thing." Barbara smiled and replied, "Oh, I want to see this." Sometimes, in rare moments God shines on us, even on this silly Irishman. Hence, the title for this picture in our calendar, "There is a God." On a lighter note, after reading this section called Sincere Thanks, the multiple divorces are no longer a mystery. Remember this is a book of lighthearted tales.

Barbara and myself at Mt Washington enjoying the afternoon sunset.

Al and Shawn and all the gang from Seacoast Harley Davidson, my buddy Bruce who when he was on the N.H. State Police was President George Bush Sr.'s bodyguard, that's pretty impressive.

The Keystone Cops and Robbers

Bruce and Peter
Their Thunder Mountain Keystone Choppers
Sandi, a true gift of friendship,
'Nice Halo' for the little Devil or Sweet Saint?
Depends on the day!

Some more of the great people in my life are the 'What's good about today' gathering in Kittery, Maine, (great group of people), Frank B., Laddie, Lynn Woods, Lynn Beach (these places gave me a refuge while I lived in the city of sin). My sponsor in the 12-step program had said: "God works through people and in your case, Peter, he works through many people keeping you out of trouble."

There was a story in the movie, 'I Am' about a man being lost in the woods, being cold, hungry and just wandering around aimlessly. Then, he noticed a cabin, "a simple basic cabin", and he knocked on the door. A man invited him in out of the freezing cold and set him down by the fire and gave him warm, dry clothes. He then brought him some hot soup and he sat nice and warm by the fire and enjoyed this hot nourishing food. He was completely happy, content, longing for nothing and just thankful for the simple basics of life. For that moment, he was free of the insatiable More, More, More mental illness that affects us all at one time or another. When you realize just how little you need, you enter a new world of freedom. I feel like that lost person who found the cabin. I am so grateful for the gift of enjoying each present moment and the simplest things of life. I enjoy what comes to me freely whether it is expensive big worldly things or just a simple cup of coffee. As every moment is equal to every other moment, so the gifts that come to me are also equal, whether expensive stuff or very simple little ones. Yes, I do possess an abundance of the worldly treasures and the key to having stuff is just not being attached to it or identifying with being the owner. I am just the caretaker of God's earthly possessions. A great saint named King Janaka had palaces, riches and '700 hundred wives'. OK, that might be just a little excessive, but he did it by not identifying himself as being a big deal and by not being attached to all the stuff.

You have to be willing to lose in order to be free. This is God's world and we are only caretakers of God's stuff. Even our children do not belong to us. *The Prophet*, Kahlil Gibran says: "Our children come through us but are not of us and not ours." They are God's children and, of course, until they are old enough we are responsible for them; but still we are just the caretakers. They are in the hands of their own karma and in God's hands. Barbara named me, The Caretaker. It seemed a fitting name.

You come into this world with no possessions and you will leave this world with no possessions. The good news is that the personal development accomplished in each lifetime goes along with our eternal soul to the next lifetime. I am eternally grateful for the wisdom of the great seers and Masters from days long ago. Their teachings can make your life an experience of health, happiness and prosperity.

I do feel that my life has been lived, in so many ways. I feel that I have already lived a long full complete life. But strangely enough, I feel that it is a long, long way from being over. It feels like this is just the beginning; in fact, another new beginning. It feels like everything from my past has come together with a cumulative effect, for the purpose of my mastering my life and mastering living in this world at this junction of time. I feel that all that work has finally paid off and I am reaping the benefits. "Our conscious practices, cause Subconscious Development," (says Ram D. R. Butler). So literally making us into a whole new person, chipping away all the false identities and revealing what was always there. It is interesting that the painter/sculptor Michelangelo said: "I saw the angel in the marble and carved until I set him free. Every block of stone has a statue inside it and it is the task of the sculptor to discover it." He also said, "The statue was already inside and I just chipped away the covering." What I have found is inside every one of us is divinity and when all the false identities fall away all that is left is our true self.

Every detail in every moment of my life is created by my thoughts and feelings. This new moment is once again a new beginning and I feel I have just come into another whole new world and a whole new even better life. This new place is somewhere that I can live in peace and contentment. I sit back and watch this world like it is an entertaining movie. This is the greatest show on Earth. I cannot stress enough that if you have any inclinations at all to do spiritual work, that you do pursue it with all your heart and mind. What will open up for you is beyond your wildest imagination and it has been right under your nose, all this time.

Learn how to use your whole mind, heart and soul as one united tool and you can't miss finding everything you desire and accomplishing all your goals. The end result of my fulfilling all my desires was that my new desire became having no desires. When all your desires are exhausted that elusive God/Happiness/Peace/Contentment will pursue you. I would not be where I am today with myself if everything (including the 'seeming' bad things and all the 'seeming' losses) had not happened exactly the way they did. In reality, I have lost nothing, nothing bad has ever happened to me. Yes, my ego has felt many losses and disappointments and even humiliation at times, but that is just my false self. I simply experienced having my karma being burnt off, which helped me head in the direction of true freedom.

I will leave you with this quote from Bob Hawes, a college professor and a great, kind and generous friend. Who has played a huge part in my completing this book: "Some come just for a season, but all come for a reason." Everything that has happened in your life, every experience positive or seemingly negative, every person that you shared karma with, it was all for your personal growth and development, leading you eventually right back to where you had begun and reuniting you with your own inner self.

Your own heart is the destination. Nowhere else to look, nowhere else to go, nothing else to do; after all your searching you will return to the place from where you started and you will know it for the first time. My true wealth is in the love that I have shared. I have come to believe and experience that there is no power greater than love.

This Sincere Thanks section could have been a book in itself and I am sure I have omitted many people that have helped me along the way.

So, once again, thanks to One and All.

Pat, John N., Myself, Brother Phil and our bikes at ThunderHaven

PREFACE

This simple book of lighthearted tales was based on my experiences over a seven-year period, while living in the historic seaport town of Newburyport, Mass. In the world there are places like Sedona, the Island of Bali, a small village in England where the electromagnet forces of the Earth cross paths, with Market Square being one of them. They create palpable energy crossroads/vortexes as explained on various PBS Series, NASA specials, Smithsonian shows and BBC science shows. One Science report from England has done research on how the foxes use the magnetic field to hunt. When one of the latest Tsunami that had devastated so much of that part of the world, the animals on these islands already knew it was coming and headed for higher terrain long before it hit. This intelligence behind Nature is the same innate Consciousness or Awareness that is within each of us. Nature's intelligence is in every cell of your body and is listening to your conscious thoughts.

This Awareness or life force is the God that we have always searched for and your own heart is God's abode. God wants to give us a win in every situation. We just need to listen. God sometimes speaks loudly, but usually speaks gently in the silence and will answer all your questions and give you precise direction for your life.

One night as I sat in Market Square, a powerful gathering spot for people and ideas in Newburyport, I realized that I was sitting in the very center of all the places that I have written about in this book. And they all had a definite direction, which was North, South, East, and West. There was the River to the North and the Old Hill Burying Ground to the South and East to the mouth of the Merrimac, The Reservation, Plum Island and the Ocean and West to Pow Wow hill, the ancient Indian burial grounds. Besides the river, Market Square was another spot where I experienced feeling a powerful pull of energy, which is not detected by the five senses. It was another of the places where the powerful energies of the Earth's forces cross. In a sense, it is a powerful intersection drawing an abundance of Earth's magnetism.

These places, like Sedona can be used to heighten your meditative experiences and to deepen your contemplation practices revealing incredible insights. You can channel your thoughts and feelings and tap into this power, aligning yourself with this ancient energy source. You can forge it into a powerful meditative and contemplation tool.

The Mystery Woman of Newburyport was one of those gifted people who could feel and tell where these places were. The Mystery Woman's name was Layne and she had taken me up along the coast of Maine to a hidden cove. This cove acted like a catch basin or sounding board for these rebounding vibrations cascading from the deeps of the ocean. At certain times, the force was incredibly palpable at these places that she showed me. I was amazed at her secret discoveries. It was not until I wrote this story that I realize I also have this gift. Actually, everyone has this gift if only they will cultivate and develop it. At first this type of gift that I was receiving seemed unbelievable to me but I quickly realized that just the way we now understand how the moon affects the tides and also how the Sun's magnetic pull affects everything, including us, it makes it easier to understand this principle.

Just because we cannot see gravity or electricity until it takes form, we do not deny its existence anymore. But, we deny this powerful unseen phenomenon and we only believe what the 'limited' five senses can tell us. The five senses only perceive about five percent of all that is actually happening. So when we tap into the subconscious mind, higher intellect and our intuition, we start experiencing the other ninety-five percent. Steven Spielberg will see the whole scene in his mind before he even starting to film. He intuitively sees the scene. So, Steven uses his intuition (his subconscious mind) to make his movies. Why it seems so foreign and overwhelming to us is because of our previous access to such a limited mindset and thinking that the five senses told the whole story. Actually, the subconscious mind (our intuition) being part of the universal mind, God/Consciousness, means it has unlimited access to knowledge. There is so much more than our limited five senses can tell us and when someone accesses what they call the sixth sense, being God, they can appear to have supernatural gifts. When in actuality, you will just be able to see the energies forming that will create the future incidents, 'like everything is in slow motion,' which is just one of the many powers an awakened person will receive. I actually used seeing this forming of the energies in my fight training and I would know what move the other fighter was about to do.

In truth, we actually don't do anything. It is the Universe that does everything. It is the only power source in this entire universe and the Universe does everything with 'ZERO' effort. All the true spiritual paths from all the ancient cultures, including the principles of Kung Fu, and even principles in the 12-step programs are all about learning how to emerge/align ourselves into the flow of this unlimited energy. They teach us how to slide out of the driver's seat and let go and let God take over. If we only would take the time to read and contemplate the ancient how-to books on this subject, we could easily become masters of creating our lives. We possess the most powerful creative device in the entire universe and that device is the mind that every individual possesses. Later on in the tale of Mysticism in Newburyport, I will share more of the wisdom of these gifts told by the ancient seekers.

I had been sober in the 12-step program for around thirty-five years at the time when I arrived in Newburyport. During this time period, I had begun reading the writings of a Meditation Master, along with the ancient teachings of the principles of truth and my life was dramatically changed forever. I had no idea that this path would bring me to a place of personal development that I did not know even existed. I was set on a whole new course of personal expansion and wonderment. I can only give an example of what the changes were like, as they were similar to the movie Star Wars, when they would hit 'Warp Drive' and take off at incredible speeds into a whole new realm; except on this path, it is the speeding up of your personal growth into a whole new world.

Like many, I started having similar experiences through grace, as the great saints, sages and seekers had written about in the ancient days. These lighthearted tales are to hopefully bring a smile to your face and possibly 'for the rare individual' to be the spark that catches your interest. Possibly making you think that maybe there is something to this 'stuff' that this silly Irishman is writing about in his tales. Actually, everyone already knows there is something to this stuff; they just are not ready to give up the outside stimulations, the quick fixes. Hopefully it will set you on your personal quest, to answer your deepest secret questions about yourself and life. Perhaps these tales will help open your eyes, ears and hopefully your heart to this Heaven on Earth, which is right here, right now if we will just be open to it. How amazing is it that we can either live in a Heaven on Earth right now or live in Hell on Earth right now and it is our choice? It truly is right under our noses and in plain sight and also absolutely everywhere. It is the 'Play of Consciousness', which is just 'God's play'. It is learning to see the game of life and the part that we are meant to play in it.

We struggle for so long, at least I did, before I finally let down my guard and let God in. It is like the boxer with his hands up protecting himself and by round fifteen he is getting very tired and starts to drop his hands and there is an opening. Now, in boxing he will get his head knocked off, but on the spiritual path, the grace of God will flow right in. All along, it had been me holding off the grace of God because of my fear and self-will. My self-will was blocking me from the unlimited grace that has always been there, just waiting for me to drop my guard 'even a little' and the grace flowed right in to change my life forever. They say that God is not only able and willing to fulfill our every desire, but is even *eager* to do so. Wow, I like that.

The secret is to align your will with God's will, which makes an unstoppable power. You can become a channel for unlimited energy and direct it into incredible accomplishments. There are people that I know who have used this principle (whether they knew they were doing it consciously or doing unconsciously) and have very successfully created amazing lives. There is only one way to be successful at anything in this life and that is through the principle of channeling this energy, whether it is for sports or success in any endeavor in this world. It is all about learning to play the game of this human existence, mastering how to use and direct this unlimited power. Or in Eastern Philosophical terms, learning to just flow with life, like the little Kung Fu master just flowing with power and grace. Another way to look at it is of being in a powerful river and just going with the current. Actually, in Star Wars, they were pretty accurate about The Force and *let the Force be with you*. It just keeps coming back to one story for me: How we align ourselves with this greater power by adding our will, so to does the Judo guy who knows how to use the power of the stronger opponent for his benefit, and he adds and aligns his strength.

For the first half of my life I tried to swim upriver against the current and literally fought everything and everyone, actually fighting myself. I wondered why I was so tired. I had met the enemy and it was myself. It is not our fault, because we need to use up a certain amount of our own self-sufficiency to get to the point that we are willing to align ourselves with the power of the universe. It is called surrendering to win.

In the 12-step program it states that we cease fighting everything and everyone, including alcohol. Everything we could ever need is present right here and right now. And even better than that, it is right within us, because *God dwells within us as us*. God is the life force that we breathe in that gives us life and then God becomes us. Our thoughts are the first and only cause of everything in our personal life. Louise Hay says: "What you think and what you believe will be true for you. Your thoughts and feelings create your life: It is that simple." I love to say to people, "What if her statement is true?" And it makes them step back and think about it. Truly, to help someone in my own small way to reconnect with his or her own inner self, would be the greatest gift I could receive.

As of late, I have come into a place with myself of happiness and complete contentment, with having a knowing of how to live. I have a feeling of already having everything I ever wanted. Having this satisfaction, it leaves me with only the purpose to help others that come into my Karmic sphere of life. God has such a sense of humor, as I was one of the most self-centered people you could find and for me to have a change of heart like this is an amazing miracle. My lifelong friend, the late Big Ben, a legendary Biker, who after his retirement from the club was to have a powerful spiritual awakening and a complete change of heart, I too am now experiencing this awakening myself. I watched him and knew that he had something I did not have at that time. Ben was known as the knock-out-king and broke many a man's jaw in his wild days and God chose to open his heart and make him a great example of God's power to change people. Ben spoke of an experience he had where he felt God literally whacked him across the back of the head, similar to St. Paul being knocked from his horse. Big Ben had such a commanding personality and always did everything in a 'big way'.

In this life, we play the role God assigns us. I have found my role and 'I play my part in this life by Just Being Myself'. My great friend, Chris Wyman, a 280-pound bodybuilder, once said: "The reason people respect your sobriety, Peter, is that most guys like you never live as long as you have or they spend their life locked up. And the reason people fear you is because you have no limits." "What do you mean by limits," I asked and Chris replied: "I rest my case, Peter, you have no idea what having any limits even means." I replied: "Why would I limit myself in any way, shape or form?"

I love all choices and of course, on this path, I would not choose to hurt anyone. But I love knowing I am free to decide how I will live my life. I do what I want to be doing all the time, naturally, not at anyone else's expense. I am someone who needs to know that what I am doing is out of my own choice; otherwise I feel trapped, depressed and can't live or even breathe.

Through Grace, 'I live the life I love and love the life I live today'. Actually, I read that back in 1977, on another friend's wall, who was also in the local riding club at the time. It was a time in my life that I was right on the fence about joining this organization. I had thought about this way of life since I was ten years old, when I had first seen pictures in Look Magazine of all the Brothers out in California riding wild and free.

I gave myself the choice at that time, I had been sober seven years, and it was finally answered, fairly quickly and without any judgment about whether it was right or wrong. What came up for me for the answer was, *I just wanted more.* I did not know what that more was going to be, but I was in for a big surprise. This riding group is accepted as an alternative lifestyle and is one of the institutions in our country today. By giving myself the choice, I was able to make the decision from my heart and was freed of the constant longing to be a part of this group of freewheeling riders. I had thought about this group on a daily basis, since 1960, from the age of ten years old and this decision freed me.

I always associated freedom with the biker lifestyle and loved the quote: 'No one tells the Wind which way to blow'. Can you imagine living with that kind of freedom? What I truly longed for was true freedom, which I was to find right within myself. True freedom comes from within, and it comes with the knowledge of your own self. This knowledge is what is called Self Knowledge. To truly be a free man in this world today is a huge accomplishment, when you have everyone wanting you to conform to his or her silly little groups, 'hooray for our group'. It is wonderful not to have to play along with someone else's dogma or their silly rituals from any of these self-serving groups. If you get your power from the group backing you up, then they can also take your power away anytime they want. I had a guy tell me; that he was coming back with a few members of a group to do a number on my brother. I calmly told him to bring as many members as he wanted, but for him to know, that they would find him stuffed in the trunk of his car. He never was to come back and that was the last we ever heard of him. That decision I had made years back about doing whatever I had to do, regarding taking care of business, give my words the conveyance of unshakeable conviction.

Nothing is free in this world, with the exception of the eternal, all sustaining life force, which can give you everything including Health, Wealth and Happiness, by just acquiring the knowledge of it.

It is all within the heart of every human being. I wanted my own power. A power that no one could take away, if I was not being a good little soldier for their cause. I did receive (really just recognized within me) this unlimited power, true freedom, complete fulfillment through grace and years of spiritual practices. Really, it was an unmerited gift from God.

It has all come together for me making it possible to live this life of freedom and independence while still being in this world, but being free of this world. When I refused to play the game of this world, by having 'no opinions', I was out and I was free. I also relinquished my need to defend my point of view and this simple decision freed up enormous amounts of energy, which in turn gave me perfect mental, physical and emotional health. The reason for most, if not all illnesses, is that we have completely drained ourselves of this life-giving energy by our continued thinking, worrying and stressing out. It is stress that makes us old. It is the stress hormone cortisol that depletes our immune system, which makes us vulnerable to illness. I do realize I quote this one a couple of times in this book, but repetition is good for really understanding something. Seventy percent of our time is spent living in the survival mode until we learn how to think correctly.

I made a decision years ago to put my health first, which meant my mental, physical, emotional and spiritual health. It was the best thing I could have ever done for myself. We all play the part we are given by God. My part is just being myself and being just one of many people that are a power of example, that individuals who are severely afflicted with alcoholism can recover and go on to have a great life. The mission I have given myself is based on the observation that most people don't recognize or have the time to appreciate all God's gifts that are given to us on a daily basis. If you give someone a gift and they really enjoy it, doesn't that make you very happy? Well we are made in God's image and nature's and I believe that my being grateful for God's gifts and giving God thanks would make God very happy. Most people are so busy just trying to survive this fast-paced life, they don't have the time to appreciate all of God's gifts and daily miracles that are so abundantly shared with us. So I have made my life's purpose to take the time and appreciate all of God's gifts to us, like sunlight, love, beauty, nature, and enjoy fully all of God's blessings. That is 'my gift' back to God. I am happy to do it for all the ones that just don't have the time. Their day will come.

Well, back at this time in Newburyport, I would sit on the boardwalk along the river, with my cup of Starbucks. And just sit and listen to the river or meditate or read some of my current lessons from Ram and I felt like the wealthiest person in the whole world. When you look at something that you consider beautiful, whether it is painting, a corvette, a sunset or a beautiful woman and you feel joy and experience happiness and love, just know that the love is not coming from the painting or the corvette or the woman. It is coming from 'your own heart'. Your own heart is the source of all love and happiness in your life. Lack of understanding causes such suffering in this world and people also suffer many other ailments, including deep loneliness. People believe that the loneliness is coming from not having another person in their life to love. The loneliness has nothing to do with another person or the love of another person. The loneliness comes from 'Not Knowing Yourself'.

Some of my happiest times are spent in long periods of fasting and solitude. And afterwards I am often reluctant to return back to the temporary world of illusion. There are many, many books telling the same truths in different ways, but for some reason a certain book will just touch the heart of an individual. There will be a special teacher that reaches deep inside you to the secret place in your heart and touches you like no one else ever had. Many paths lead to the top of the mountain, and there are many spokes in the wheel that connect to the same hub. I don't think my little book of tales is meant to be for very many, but I do believe that there is some rare individual for whom these tales will remind them of their own past and their own greatness. I have tried with honesty and openness to share my joys and struggles in this life that I have lived and hope it is of benefit to someone. My dear friend, Sandi, after reading the book, told me that she loved the book and it truly touched her heart. So, this book is a complete success already with the touching of just one special heart.

My great friend Kay Butler, who has been a Godsend for me during these last couple of big growth periods, has shown me techniques on how to write. Which are to write for myself, as if I am just journaling and also how writing from love is the most powerful way to write. So, I sit quietly and breathe and get myself in a good place, before I write so my dark side does not play into it. Yes, I have or had quite the dark side, but it seems to have been arrested and put to sleep?

Another reason for this book is just to encourage those who think they cannot achieve what they would love to have in this lifetime. There is *always hope* and *we can achieve whatever our hearts truly desire.* You just need the right tools. Always remember, if you are still breathing, you are still in the ballgame and miracles can happen in a moment and at any moment and everything can change rapidly. So hang in there and be open to learn about the empowering principles of truth. Are you ready for the adventure of a lifetime?

I cannot encourage you enough to learn about the Mind. One of the things that has become so clear to me is that *it is all about the mind.* Your mind can be your best friend or your mind can be your worst enemy. Your own mind will be the source of all happiness and it also will be the source of all your troubles, if you let it run free. 'We' want to run free, but we don't want our minds running like a wild horse out of control. Controlling your mind is the most important thing in regards to controlling your life. In the back of this book will be a number of books full of easily assimilated knowledge about the mind. People think when they begin a true spiritual path that it is going to be all fun and games. Nothing could be further from the truth, your whole being will be rearranged and you will go places you never expected. And finally you will arrive at the place where you will see 'The True Purpose of Life' and you never will be the same again.

I will be eternally grateful for the knowledge of Right Understanding. When you know yourself, you know other people. You will actually know everyone, as there is only one mind, only one set of human behaviors, only one set of basic instincts. And when you understand them you can see clearly what people are up to. You will know what they are going to do, long before they do it. Once again, it makes knowing or seeing the future very obvious. I was someone that you could get to react violently just by mentioning something from the past. I was 'easily manipulated with a few words'. It is called the 'reactive mind' and you can see evidence of it all day long with people reacting to other's words or actions automatically, without any conscious decisions. People have no defenses if they are in the state of the reactive mind and can be easily manipulated by people.

One of my motivations to gain knowledge was my ego hated it when someone knew more about me than I did of myself and then they would give me that sly smile. The real problem was not them, of course, but it was my own lack of understanding of myself and of most things of life. I had learned in the 12-step program that it is not people, places or things and that when I am bothered, it is always me. People may actually be doing the negative things you perceive, but you can only change yourself, through correcting your thinking.

Well, back to the point of this section and that is we can live an extraordinary life of Health, Happiness, Abundance, Prosperity, and Fulfillment. We can have success in everything we do, experience Unconditional Love, basically having all life has to offer. It is our choice. One day, I saw that if I live my life like I took a vow of poverty, thinking it was making me more spiritual, I would not receive any more brownie points on the path. And that if I lived with enjoying all the comforts and pleasures of the world, while I was here doing my spiritual practices, it would make 'no difference' in the final outcome either. So there is no reason not to enjoy all the pleasures of this world, as they too are actually a part of God. The one (God) has become everything and everyone, excluding nothing, so what is there to renounce? The trick is not being identified with the stuff or attached to it, that gives you freedom from it, allowing you to enjoy what your human side likes while we are here. One day I thought to myself I am living right now in a huge beautiful home, with a collection of exceptional custom cycles, living with the perfect lover, mentor, best friend, for that period of karma, along the coast of Southern Maine. And literally, I was living with having all the comforts and pleasures of the material world, living like a millionaire and all I did was Think Good Thoughts to create all this.

In the Peter Pan movies, Peter shows the children how to fly and the secret to flying was 'Thinking Happy Thoughts'. I thought, it is true, because all I did was, 'Just Think Great Thoughts', and think about what my heart truly desired and I got what I thought about. I got every single thing that I wanted when I used this technique, for the past twenty-five years. We so underestimate our own mind, because we don't realize that we literally direct Universal Consciousness with our thoughts. People would laugh and say that it could not be that simple. And I say: "Just give it a fair try and see for yourself." I am living proof that it is just that simple, what you think is what you get. If you honestly take a look at your life, you will see you are living basically what you expected, what you thought life would be. "The outcome is spontaneously contained in the expectation. What you expect influences the outcome," is a quote from Deepak Chopra. Ram Butler had said, "I no longer like to leave the results of anything up to chance; I see how it will end before I begin." That quote of Ram's is just one of the many priceless pieces of wisdom that Ram has shared in his teachings.

When I first read about creative thought and how you get what you think about, I knew it was true. Negative, limited thoughts from the first part of my life had always manifested for me and became my life. I believed life was tough and I only could get a half decent job, a half decent relationship, a half decent car, and a half decent motorcycle. When I looked at my life, I knew 'I never got less'. 'I got exactly what I expected and believed'. I thought, what do I have to lose and I started correcting my thinking and thinking health, happiness, success in everything I do, abundance, prosperity and thinking about all the good things of life.

It started changing almost immediately for me and for the past twenty-five years I have lived with having it all. So 'I Know' that this principal: What You Think Is What You Get is the absolute truth and the most important thing any human being can learn. Your mind can create anything and if you are not watching your mind, who knows what will get created. We are creating in every moment and we all are like little Gods creating our lives. People will say that is nonsense, and for them it is nonsense, because what they believe will be true for them. Henry Ford said: "If you believe you can that will be true for you, or if you believe you can't that will be true for you." So which do you want? Really, could it be that simple? Yes, I know without a doubt this is the absolute truth, try it and find out for yourself.

I love to say: "What do you have to lose by trying it?" I not only believe this, but I know in my heart without the slightest doubt that my thoughts are the first cause of everything in my life. And if I direct my thoughts into what I truly desire, it will be 'compelled to physically manifest'. Wow, how powerful is that and how lucky I am to have this knowing and conviction of this principle as part of my own consciousness and being? Today, it is literally who I am. My sponsor in the 12-step program told me that spiritual food is processed like regular food. We chew it up, swallow it, digest it and then it becomes part of us. It becomes who we are, just as food becomes your body. All it takes is the willingness to read and reread and reprogram our subconscious mind to a healthy state.

The willingness to read and reread these principles of truth will automatically change your hard drive. Your conscious practices, reading the principles of truth, meditation, solitude, cause 'Subconscious Development' and literally reprogram your mind. The scientists today believe your mind is just like a computer and can be reprogramed from the limited misconceptions to healthy ways of thinking and living. That even Universal Consciousness is like a massive computing system, working just the same way.

This has been my experience for the past twenty-five years of receiving everything I wanted by using these techniques. It is so simple a principle that most are blind to it. Everyone wants big answers, "What are we all from Texas?" And we miss what is readily available in these incredible simple gifts of knowledge and wisdom. The 12-step programs talks of, the key of willingness opening the inner doors of the program and this has been true for me as my world opened up, with a decision to go all the way. But I must say that it was through right understanding that I gained my freedom and independence. I had misconceptions of life and myself and I was boxed in a small world, loaded with limited negative thinking. I replaced it with the Principles of Truth that have been around since the beginning of time. Your environment and the people you have in your life are very important. If you want to continue to grow and have a great life, you need like-minded people heading in the same direction as you. Earlier in my life, I had got stuck in a negative environment and surrounded myself with people who were equally negative and stuck and we all just complained and we went nowhere, year after year. I wanted more and got out of that environment and moved on to a great life. I am so glad I did, as most of those people are still stuck in the same spot, forty years later. Thank You God for opening my mind, heart and eyes. The people that you surround yourself with can be just like the crabs in the following story which goes like this: They say you do not have to put a lid on the can of crabs, because if one tries to climb out, the other crabs pull him back down. Just like the gangs in New York, if someone wants to better himself and maybe go to college, they all turn on him. Once again, the same old story about human nature, so you really want to surround yourself with healthy, like-minded people.

I choose to believe in choices, in health, happiness, prosperity, abundance and freedom. So the point of this little spiel of mine is that we truly have a choice, as does 'every human being, in every moment'. We have a choice of whether to have a mundane life; of being born, going to school, growing up, getting a job, getting married, buying a house, growing old and then one day dying and never having really lived; or, we can choose an extraordinary life for ourselves full of health, happiness, abundance, success, fulfillment, prosperity, wisdom and unconditional love. The list of gifts just goes on and on. The amazing prayer called the Serenity prayer is as follows: God grant me the serenity to accept the things I cannot change; Courage to change the things I can; And wisdom to know the difference. The problem can occur when someone lacking the knowledge of having choices, because of their misconception about their own power, accepts things that they could have easily changed. Misconceptions of a lifetime can keep you stuck and make you a helpless, powerless victim. That is why right understanding of yourself and life are so important.

Another one of the things that plagues people is their caring what others think of them. This is truly one of the greatest gifts I have received from following this path: I don't care what anyone thinks of me or what they think about my life or theirs. When you finally see that if everyone thinks I am wonderful, it does not make my life any better and if everyone thinks I am terrible, it does not affect my life in the least, either. So you can just forget about praise or blame and just regard it as inconsequential.

Yes, it does take the willingness of doing the work and the repetition of these simple, but powerful principles of truth. And so does everything else in this life that is worthwhile, including sports, success in business, or mastery in any trade. All it takes is the right attitude with repetition with the appropriate tools for the task at hand. It is so worth it though. And, in the beginning it will take a guide to help get you started and who will lead you back to your own heart, which then becomes 'your infallible guide' for the rest of your journey. How cool is that? If you are not completely happy with your life, the tools to change everything about yourself and your life are in every bookstore, ashram, spiritual center and library.

I wish you health, happiness, prosperity and success in whatever you choose. And that includes even if you choose not to try these suggestions at this time, as I do not believe in right or wrong anymore. If something here is helpful for you great and if nothing here floats your boat that is great too.

I wish you well.

I do hope this book of tales will at least bring a smile to your face and a good laugh, at this silly, slightly eccentric, Irish seeker.

This picture is of my 120 Race Road Glide

INTRODUCTION

This, basically, is just the story of another soul's reawakening in this particular lifetime and his experiences during that time. I have always said there is something magical about writing stuff out. Writing will give you a clear perspective and insights on whatever subject that you desire to know the hidden truth about. It is like God is talking directly to us as we write. I used this principle in regards to a situation I had in the 12-step program when I was twenty years sober. As, the incredibly helpful sponsor I had at that time began to forget who he was and revert back to the angry, resentful, egotistical individual that he had been in the past. Once again, he returned to blaming people, places and things for his problems. I carried anger towards him for a period of time, until I saw my sweetheart at the time (Bobbie Joe, an incredible woman and friend) and discovered she had gotten free of her resentments. I asked her what she had done and she said that she had written out her experience with this sponsor and that particular group, in the way you would do a fourth step in the program.

I instantly knew it would work and realized I could use this technique for a lot more than just getting rid of the past baggage. I would use it in a journaling-type process for anything that was going on in my life. I sat down and started writing out exactly how I felt and almost immediately realized my anger was 'really disappointment'. My sponsor had been enormously helpful in the beginning twenty years, and when he reverted back to the mixed-up individual he had been when he entered the program, I was disappointed. 'My disappointment was disguised as anger'. When I saw the truth of this the anger fell away and I wished him well. I was never to even think about him or the past situation again. I love my freedom from useless baggage.

The past is the past, acknowledge it and then let it go mentally, just forget about it. It then will be time to move on. Someone made the statement that I probably would not be sober if it were not for my sponsor. That was nonsense. I was reaching out for help to get sober and God always answers despair and any number of people could have provided me with what I needed, possibly even better. I felt badly for this individual and his lack of understanding. I was through drinking when I came to the program, so God could have worked through any number of people to help me. I always give all the credit to God. Naturally, we are grateful for people being the vehicle/messenger for God's grace, but I would be foolish to take credit for any good that might flow through me to another. My part is just being willing to be the messenger and if God chooses to use me that is great. I always know that the source of help is God and not this silly Irishman. It is God working through people and when you forget that fact, then the trouble with your ego starts. I have watched better people than me get off the track by forgetting that it is God working through people. They started thinking they are the source and that was the beginning of their downfall, as was the case with my sponsor. I wish health, happiness and prosperity to him and everyone (there have been many) that have helped me on my journey.

If someone sincerely reaches out, God will work through people to give them exactly what he or she needs. The source of where over-dependence comes from is by giving credit where credit is not due, putting people up on pedestals. It is one reason people get stuck in their personal development and never grow. There are examples of that with whole recovery groups of people that are over dependent and still stuck thirty or forty years later, whining and blaming others for their problems. They continue to live in fear of their alcoholism when there is true recovery and freedom from this fatal illness. They choose to never take responsibility for themselves. Always remember that individuals come and go and individuals also often fail, but the principles of truth of an authentic path, like the 12-step program Never Fail. Principles of truth are eternal. So, always look to the principles and don't over-depend on any individual, groups or institutions. It has been a painful lesson for me to learn, but a priceless gift of freedom.

I would liked to have taken the easier way out and always look to another, but it was my time to take it to the next level of freedom by taking responsibility for my life. Actually, I felt I was forced into growing up and went kicking and screaming at least at first. It is so much easier to be the child and look to someone else but to acquire the freedom I desired, I had to finally take responsibility for my life and myself. What you focus on becomes true for you. And, if you focus on being a sick alcoholic with this all-powerful illness that has total control over you and how badly you are affected by it, you will unnecessarily remain badly affected by it. And it will continue to have control over you even twenty, thirty, forty years or even more. You will live your life as a victim and a sick person. That will be their choice. People make their illness into their God and put their faith in the illness. They will speak of the illness almost with a reverence and a kind of kneeling before it.

But if you choose to put your faith in God and the recovery program and know that the program works. And that you can recover and arrest your illness, then you will recover and arrest your illness and become a healthy individual. What you believe will be true for you and I choose to believe that the 12-step program works and that you can recover and arrest your illness and live a normal, healthy, prosperous life. So that is the live I life, just because I believe it and was willing to do the work. These teachings are not for the newcomer in the 12-step program, but for the one that has gotten their feet firmly planted on the ground and in a good spiritual condition. From that position someone can take their personal development to new heights of freedom and independence. The reason I believe this fact (what you think is what you get) is because the first part of my life was very hard and it was exactly as I believed and expected my life to be. When I simply changed my view of life and myself, everything changed and I entered into a great new world. I still am in awe that it could be that simple: Change your thoughts, and change your life.

I know in my heart that what guarantees my sobriety is my continued spiritual expansion, not some individual or group. I have benefitted so much by writing stuff out that I cannot help but keep repeating that: Writing stuff out is magical. My story begins in the town of Lynn, Mass. This was the place where the toughest period of my karma was to be burnt off. My spiritual journey really began at age nineteen when I entered the halls of the 12-step program for alcoholism and quickly had a spiritual awakening. In the Yogic traditions it says that there are seventeen levels of intensity of the inner awakening called Shaktipat and I had my awakening on a lower level of intensity, but nonetheless it was my awakening at that time. It would be twenty-five years later that I was introduced to a yogic spiritual path and almost immediately experienced a much more intense and higher level of awakening that changed me forever.

In the 12-step program, it talks of a spiritual awakening and also a spiritual experience; many will experience both, as did the founder of the program and myself. My spiritual awakening was when I was to realize that a power greater than myself had removed the obsession for alcohol and drugs. This awakening was responsible for the beginning of a long painful process of having my eyes and my mind open about myself in ways I had never experienced in life before. Five years sober, I experienced the worst year of my life. When my thinking shifted from being in the program because I wanted to be there, to I had to be there, I was instantly trapped. I am someone whose freedom and independence is the most valuable possession I have and I need to know I am doing what I want to be doing or I become a trapped animal. I was as trapped as anyone could possibly be trapped in the physical world and 'it was all in my mind', due to a misconception I had formed with the help of my sponsor and the group I was in at the time.

I learned a powerful lesson about the power of thoughts, beliefs, conceptions and 'misconceptions' at that time. I learnt that my body would respond and react to something that I only believed in my mind, equally to something that was actually happening for real on the outside. This was a priceless lesson that I was to use right up to the present time. There is a part of the brain called the limbic that cannot tell the difference between you or another or whether it is really happening or only exists in your mind. It also can't tell whether something is going out or coming in and this part of the brain will give you the experience first of what you are wishing for someone else. So whatever you are wishing for someone else, your brain will give you the experience first. And it will give you the experience of whatever you believe. That is why when you wish ill will towards another you are the one that will suffer.

During that fifth year I hung on by my fingertips and lost everything outward in my life except the most important thing, my sobriety. I took walks in Lynn Woods everyday with my snub-nose thirty-eight in my pocket and a Raven twenty-five automatic strapped to my ankle and my favorite Buck knife in my back pocket. And, I also took long walks on the beach. It saved my sanity. At that time, I lived in a constant war zone in my mind. When we spend time in Nature we are very close to God and the reason we feel good in Nature is that 'Our inner nature is the same as Nature and the same as the intelligence behind Nature, which is God'. That intelligence behind Nature is in every cell of our bodies and 'listens and obeys our conscious thoughts'. In Nature we return home to our true self and feel at peace. One day, as I walked along the reservoir as the afternoon sunset lit up the water, which I called Sunset Boulevard, I had my first spiritual experience. It was extremely profound. I had a clear and unshakeable knowing in my heart and my mind that God was the 'Intelligence behind Nature', that power that controlled the planets, the seasons and us. And I knew it was not different from my own nature.

I knew that God was not some bearded man up in the clouds that would punish me for not worshiping him. Even as a child that idea of a vengeful God never made sense to me. Really, God was going to strike down a child with a lightning bolt for not bowing before him. As I write, I keep flashing back to being in Church and getting physically sick. I now know that they were trying to force feed me teachings that I did not believe and I keep throwing them up. I knew way back then, that the God they presented was not the true God, but a manmade story to control people. Thank God for the truth. That intelligence behind Nature (God) is in every cell of my body, even the most infinitesimal smallest cell and 'it responds deeply to my feelings'. Feelings are a language that the Universe understands. Through my thoughts and feelings I have direct conscious communion with God. From that moment, I knew I was one with God.

There is only one source (God) and from that one source everything and everyone has emerged. We exist for a while and then we are all drawn back into that source. So, nothing really happened except

God's play, 'The Play of Consciousness'. When I could see this was not really my life but just an extension of the grace of God, for whatever his or her purpose, it changed everything. Now that does not mean that while I am here I don't enjoy the pleasures of the physical world. They are all God's creations, too. I certainly love the touch and company of a woman and riding my custom cycles up in the mountains, but it is the realization of knowing for myself what is really important in this life, which is Love. And we each have to find our own place and purpose. The only one that knows the answers for you is your own inner self, who you will find is the God you have always searched for and is right in your own heart.

There is only one God, one power and when I saw that the power that flowed through my hands to help an elderly woman across the street or the energy that flowed through my hands to do something destructive was the same energy, it made me aware of there being only one source of power and also to be conscious of how I use God's power. God's power flows through you in your thoughts, words, deeds and attitude and becomes your life and your world. So, it is always good to think before you act, which took me a lifetime to learn. With great power comes great responsibility. When you realize you can uplift and make someone's day with a few kind words or you can ruin someone's day with a few unkind words, it makes you more cautious with your words. People have a hard enough time as it is in this life, without us making things harder for them by our words or actions. That really touched my heart and I try to live by it.

My heart has reopened today and this is why I believe so strongly in the power of God. God's love has overridden the intense, fearful, cold-hearted side of my nature. I was someone who felt nothing for anyone else, completely self-consumed, like a psychopath or sociopath. I have watched so-called friends die in front of me and I remained emotionless. Being a very supersensitive child and having gotten my feelings hurt by being laughed at for being different, my heart was to close at a very young age. Not long after my heart closing at twelve years old, I was to experience what having a closed heart really meant, for the first time, as I watched someone as they bled out after having been shot and felt nothing, totally unaffected and completely emotionally shutdown. Somewhere along the way, I had to admit to myself, I really was missing a piece of humanity; I had no guilt for anything. I was lacking a conscience. I really could not see any use for a conscience, at that time. Today, it is so obvious how a little psycho is created or developed. The pain and lack of love is what creates these individuals. I watched and saw what scared people, for instance, if in a fight you went for their eyes. The thought of someone going for their eyes, more than anything else, would just horrify them. So, the person that grew up feeling like he had no power was finding powerful tools for his survival. I know today that an imbalance in the fight-or-flight reaction in my body (which the Biochemist say is the cause of alcoholism) put me in this mood all the time, even though it could be very subtle.

The good news and the miracle is that today my heart is wide open and I look to make people's life easier. And also, I am slower to speak today. My friend, Big Ben use to say; be slow to speak and quick to listen. This is a little of topic but I just love these two statements; A smart person learns from his mistakes but a wise person learns from 'other's mistakes'. That is one of the gifts that will start happening for you after an awakening. The other statement, which certainly helps keep my big ego down to right size, is; Even a broken clock 'is right twice a day'.

I probably still have both sides, these darker sides of me, which seem to be at rest, as I choose to live in the light. It is not out of virtue, but it is from loving the feeling of being truly alive and feeling love within myself. And when there is only one, then if you hurt someone or the planet you are really hurting yourself and eventually you will suffer. My father asked me one time, "Do you ever think before you do something?" I thought about it for a minute and said, "No." So, who was captaining my ship? That would be the reactive mind at that time and the source of all my self-made troubles.

In the 12-step book, it speaks of the purpose of the writing of that book and it was to help people find a God of their own understanding. Well, that could be another title of this book, *Finding the God of your understanding* or as Marianne Williamson's book was called, *A Return to Love*, or this book could be called *A Book of Remembrance*. I will just stick with *Mysticism in Newburyport*, a book of lighthearted tales.

There were many growth periods along the way, mostly very painful. Eventually I had worked through the worst and was to begin experiencing a very amazing lifestyle. And it really took off when I arrived in the Newburyport area. So, these stories are mainly about what was to follow, after reading my first book by a Meditation Master. My life was to be changed forever and it was another seven-year cycle of my journey. My life has been a series of these seven-year periods, always culminating in ending up in a whole new even better world and also surprisingly, surviving another whirlwind bout of karma.

As I sit writing these tales in York Harbor, Maine, I have just come out of another seven-year cycle of my life and more insights and revelations just keep coming. I thought today that God does everything; we only mistakenly think we are doing this stuff. And on top of that, God does everything with 'zero effort'. Yes, I know I have repeated that one, so have you got it? If this is true, why in the world do we waste our energy making it harder by getting in God's way? So, for me to try or struggle is silly. All I need do is see and feel how I want things to be and then just suit up and show up and play the appropriate role, like an actor. When someone would be telling Jeff and Chris, my friends from Newburyport and myself how great they were, big Chris would smile and say, 'Sure, I will play along'. Such wisdom, learn to just play along and you will live a lot longer.

Well, it's time to begin the writing of these lighthearted tales.

'Wish you the best'
The All Thunder Clubhouse

The All Thunder Clubhouse

THE EARLY YEARS

This story begins with my being born an Irish Catholic down in Lynn, Mass., on December 7, 1950. You will see very quickly how the seven-year cycles have been a regular occurrence in my life, starting with seven years in Catholic schools. I did not do very well in that school system and I think they were glad to see me go. They say in the Eastern Philosophical teachings that we will choose a certain amount of stuff, Karma, to burn off in each lifetime and that we will also pick our parents, who will treat us in a way that corresponds to our subconscious impressions. I fortunately picked the perfect parents for me and they played their part perfectly at that time and place for my individual development. I am sincerely grateful for all that they provided me and for the patience and unconditional love, that they consistently showed my brothers and me.

Thankfully, my father was a gentle soul, truly a good man, who did not have my personality. He was someone that you could truly say had the patience of a saint. I am actually overjoyed that I am finally starting to exhibit some of his qualities, after a lifetime of my own spiritual work. My mother also played her part perfectly and treated me exactly as I had conceived myself to be and because of our relationship I was to burn off huge pieces of my karma, my issues. I am sincerely grateful for her today, as the knowledge from the principles of truth has explained it all to me and also freed me from any ill feelings of my childhood.

If it were not for the two of them being exactly as they were, I would have never worked through my low self-esteem and complete lack of self-confidence issues. They fully provided for me and kept me safe. I am very grateful for that. How fortunate I was to be born into a family that treated me so humanely, as I could have easily found myself in serious trouble because of the way I was at that time. I felt like a tortured, trapped animal most of my life and would viciously turn on you in a heartbeat, which was just all fear-based behavior. I knew nothing of love and lived in a world in my mind that was consumed with fear and hate. I would watch gang members who had love for their brothers and they were much healthier than me, as I felt nothing for no one. It was sixty-six years ago that I was born and the lifelong friend who was born in the hospital at the same time was just arrested this year again, on numerous felony charges. Still today, he lives the lifestyle of the Outlaw Biker. It is interesting, especially with us living so much longer, to watch the people we have karma with. I have watched many of the guys I rode motorcycles with as far back as the sixties that at that time did not get into riding clubs. But many of them are now joining clubs in their late sixties and even seventies.

Today, in this world, and especially in the motorcycle world, everyone is joining some type of support group or forming some alliances. Everyone is picking sides and everyone is packing weapons. This world has truly reverted back to the tribe mentality, and back to different types of survival groups. Just take a look around or watch the news and see one group after another forming, ready to fight to protect their special interests. I also considered, in the last couple years, of aligning myself deeper with a certain group in the riding world, as my family and friends have always been involved with it. But I have chosen to have my faith in the God that has always taken care of me so completely, and not any group. The highways today have become so organized and controlled by key members of certain groups and these key players have their gopher clubs doing their bidding. They know everyone that rides, in any particular area. So they know whether to steal from them or to know if they are a threat. You see, once again, people coming from basic survival instincts. It is similar to prison today, as an individual, no matter how strong they are, they cannot survive alone in lockup. He or she ends up becoming a part of some group or a so-called brotherhood.

I remember watching as John Gotti, the Teflon Don, the head of the mafia, went into prison. He had to pay protection to the white supremacists, to stay alive in lockup. Really, the head of New York organized crime had to pay protection, isn't that ironic? It is all about the numbers. If you watch a nature show, many times after the lion, king of the Jungle, makes a kill, the hyenas will drive him away and take his food, because of the overwhelming numbers of the hyenas. Once again, we see how every human being has the basic animal behaviors and without the opening of the higher energy places, chakras, in our heart region, we tend to live by basic instincts. These basic human tendencies are for sex, power and control, which you will see all through this life and this world.

So, back to the story of my childhood, which for the most part was a nightmare. If it were not for Lynn Beach, Lynn Woods and our camping trips to the White Mountains and being in Nature, I would never have survived. One of the most powerful memories I have as a child was at ten years old. It was late at night, when I awoke to the roar of engines just outside my bedroom window. I went to the window and I saw motorcycles lined up across the entrance of the street and watched my brother pull out from the pack and ride up to the house. Then each rider turned his bike and headed off into the night. I still get goose bumps running up my spine, just thinking about it. For me it represented power, freedom and a sense of brotherhood. It touched something deep inside of me, possibly of remembrances of past lives of living a warrior lifestyle.

As a child I felt very powerless, very out of place and different. When at ten years old, in 1960, I saw pictures in Look Magazine of the Bike Club from California and their freewheeling lifestyle; I knew that riding would be the life that I would choose. Lynn, after Lowell, Mass., was one of the places that this new club was gaining members and you could hear the preaching of this brotherhood. It is kind of ironic that as a kid I would get physically sick in the Catholic Church with their preaching, but across the street, I would sit on the stoop of the barroom with the bikes and listen to the preaching of this brotherhood and be so uplifted. There was a song back then, by The Animals, of a warm San Franciscan night and Angels young and old were feeling all right. I can feel and picture that so clearly, like I was there. This philosophy of life and riding has become a way of thinking about life that many of us have adopted and it is still true for me today.

Below is a picture of Wolf Man, who was an x-marine, biker and heavyweight boxer. Wolf man, another great friend, has also passed on. I am there driving the bike, my 'stroker' Harley Panhead chopper, and my brother Philip and back in the early sixties.

1965

My oldest brother, Skip, (who was a Master Craftsman) was a powerful influence in my life, as I followed him from a young age into drinking, then the drugs of the sixties, weight training and boxing, motorcycle riding, then meeting the original members of the riding club that was forming a local chapter, and later into the 12-step program and then finally, into the study and practice under a spiritual Master. At fifteen, my oldest brother, Skip took me to a Rocky's type gym in Boston and I was immediately hooked on physical training, weightlifting, boxing and martial arts. I have trained more than 50 years in different training styles. My teenage years were of excessive drinking and drug use. These years were one of my seven-year cycles and also lots of trouble. In a very short period of time, I had experienced seven broken noses, a fractured skull, head split open, concussions, front teeth kicked out by a Lynn cop, high-speed chases on motorcycles and cars, numerous car wrecks, bike crashes, being shot at by cops, occasionally returning 'the favor' and all the stuff that is just business as usual in a place like Lynn. All that behavior was just accepted as a normal way of life.

One experience of mine that will illustrate the personality change of an alcoholic when they take a drink is in the following story. When I was fifteen, I was someone that was so painfully shy, that I could hardly raise my hand in class to answer a question. During summer vacation I had been drinking every day with my cousin Tom and a friend, who both have since left this world. And we ended up stealing a car. As, we pulled up alongside a guy walking on the sidewalk; I opened the door and grabbed him. I slammed his head on the side of the car a few times and then dragged him into the back seat and robbed him.

That was the last thing I remembered, as I was experiencing an alcoholic blackout. The next thing I realized was that we were going over the George Washington Bridge in New York and we had been driving all night. We had forced our hostage to drive. The little Catholic schoolboy, who could not even raise his hand in class, was doing all these actions with seemingly no problem and I never even remembered them. Alcoholism is truly a serious, deadly illness, if not treated, but anyone can fully recover. It happens, by becoming aware of the Grace of God coming into your life. There would have been a whole list of felonies for just this one night of my drinking. Since I was fifteen years old, I probably would have gotten off lightly, as I was considered a minor. I do have a vague memory of that night, and it was of being in White Plains, New York, sometime during the night and being in a fist fight with my cousin on the front lawn of a State Trooper's home. We had broken into his police car and stole his gun and hat. The fight was over the hat.

The next morning, in Greenwich Village, the alcohol had worn off and I was back to the runny-nose, 15-year-old kid and like usual, I had an ungodly hangover. They say, that alcoholism is an allergy to alcohol and that rings true with me because of how sick I would be after a drunk. We spent some time in Greenwich Village and then started the awful journey home and it would be time to face the consequences, once again, for my actions. The term 'life sucks' really applied to my life at that time. So, this was just one of many of these episodes of insanity, during this time frame.

In 1968, I was in a house in East Lynn and there were 'seven' of us and the group was made up of bikers, major drug dealers, armed robbers and myself. Over the years, one by one, they died off and when I went to the funeral for the fifth guy that had been at the house that night, I met the other last remaining person from that party. He was a three-hundred-pound biker, who is on the History Channel's *Gangland* series. He also was dying, as he was full of cancer. It was interesting to watch as his bodyguard (who was strutting around so full of pride for being chosen and having the honor to escort him, as this biker was a legend in the motorcycle world) did not even see the look in his eyes, which was telling the story of a very hard life and of his knowing that it soon would be over.

As the bikers were leaving, he turned and made eye contact with me. We exchanged nods and I was to look deep into his eyes and right into his soul. It sent a chill up my spine. I knew we had been connected many, many times in past lives. He was another person that I had known since we were kids and he also would be gone soon. We never spoke that night, just exchanged nods and then we got on our motorcycles and headed in different directions down the road, very different directions as it has turned out.

He died shortly afterward and once again I was the lone survivor from another group of associates. I never thought about that group from that house again, until one night when I was training at Hard Nocks Gym and on the radio came the same song that played that day in East Lynn, in 1968. It was Jimmy Hendricks 'Crosstown Traffic'. *I thought I am the only one left from that motley crew of seven bandits.* And once again I experienced another chill up my spine.

Sometimes I wonder why I am still here and so many others are already gone. I came to the conclusion that this present lifetime of mine is just my time to grow and master these principles of life. My life could have been over a number of times, with my behavior and actions. I believe we all have, in different lifetimes, have taken lives and also have died very young, so none of that is really a big deal. But the time comes for us, that we will have a purposeful life and actually experience some personal development. It reminds me of the saying, "Lynn, Lynn, the city of sin, you never come out the way you went in." The next story basically tells the whole story of my life during that time period and it was just one of many troubled nights.

After a night of drinking and drugging, I rolled my 68 Dodge Charger RT, 440-magnum muscle car onto the main road and slammed the gas pedal to the floor. It just lifted up with the traction bars and from the gripping of the huge racing slicks, and we took off. A couple miles down the road, the Lynn and Saugus cops had set up a roadblock, 'for some safecrackers' and when we approached, at over a hundred miles an hour, they just started shooting. I slammed the throttle deeper into the floorboards and that beast responded with even more power. I just loved that feeling of a high-performance machine, just exploding with power. I can remember that feeling like it was yesterday. Those muscle cars of the sixties were really something special.

A mile down the road we took a left turn at seventy miles an hour and the wheels on the left side of the car came right off the ground. All the while, the guys were throwing guns, drugs and booze out the windows. If we had gone straight down the road, we would have met up with the State Police, who were waiting for us on Rte. 1. I am sure they were loaded for bear. We took the back roads home that no one really used at night, because a few weeks earlier someone had dumped the body of a police informant along the side of the road, with his head cut off. No surprise, there was not much traffic on these roads at night. It is interesting that right around the same time they found a second body, with the head cut off, over in East Boston. All it got was a little write-up on a back page of the newspaper.

I got up the next day and had forgotten all about the happenings of that previous night, until a friend called and said: "Keep that car hidden and out of sight, the cops are looking everywhere for you. There is a front-page write-up of you and your hoodlum friends." The front page of the evening paper had said: "High speed chase with safecrackers. Police from two towns emptied their guns into the getaway car as they ran the roadblock." Sounds more like a story about Bonnie and Clyde than little old me.

I thought I had better go look in the trunk to see if we had a safe stuffed in there, as I did not remember much of that night. It might have been us? I will never know, having been in an alcoholic blackout for most of the night. So this was how things went for me at that time in my life. I was just going out for a few drinks, just take the edge off of life. I am sure you would have wanted to spend time with me, back then.

At the time I had a suspended jail sentence out at Deer Isle in Boston Harbor for a narcotics and conspiracy conviction in Boston. And the boys from Boston really don't like the guys from Lynn. I would have been really outnumbered, and this Irish boy would have been in the minority in this Boston prison. Once again, the grace of God saved my ass. Despite all the criminal acts that I was usually 'unconsciously' involved with during this period, I was arrested and caught only once. And it really was the grace of God, because of this narcotics and conspiracy conviction the military did not want any part of me. So I missed the Vietnam War because of this fluke arrest.

Another example, of how I lived back then was when I got a phone call from one of the guys. His name was Mark T. and he was a prospect for the riding club. He said that he had gotten an early release from prison for 'good behavior' and would I pick him up in East Boston? I laughed to myself, and I knew he had escaped somehow, but I said: "Sure I will be right over." I jumped on my bike and headed to town. I knew he would be there for me if I was in a similar situation and we always take care of our own. There is a code of brotherhood with Lynn associates. We hit speeds of 120 mph coming across the stretch of road called the Lynn Marsh. And when we hit a rise in the road, we were actually airborne for a little while. We rolled into Lynn and were safe in the badlands, once again.

Mark (a major player in the drug world) was arrested a few days later and back in the big house. Mark's new Hemi Charger and Harley Chopper sat idle waiting for his return. Mark was another friend that heroin took at a young age. Another friend, whose road name was Peco, who belonged to the riding club, also succumbed to the drugs around the same time. My cousin, Lenny came back from Vietnam with a bad heroin addiction and began robbing banks. In one of the bank robberies, they shot a cop on the way out of the bank and that got him a long prison sentence. He too, died young from the heroin. The list just grows longer and it is part of the reason why I am trying to finish this book. Who knows how much time, any of us have?

The guys I grew up with all had muscle cars - Corvettes, Hemi Chargers, GTO's, Hemi Barracudas, and 440 Road Runners - and many a night we would be out drinking and road racing. One particular night, we got drinking and drugging and decided to go road racing. The problem was that we had shopping bags full of kilos of 'recreational drugs' in all the cars. We looked like we just came from the supermarket after doing the family grocery run. The whole pack of us ended up going through downtown Wakefield, Mass., at over a hundred miles an hour. It would be fair to say we all had pretty poor judgment at that time in our lives. The good news is that it was the drugs of the sixties, which were grass, hash, psychedelics, crystal meth (the bikers concoction) and it was all about partying. I was to watch it all change in the seventies, when the cocaine and heroin really took off. The drug cartels started letting the heroin come through in a more potent form, so you could snort it and did not have to get involved with needles. It quickly became the cool thing to do, even among the upper class professionals and even school kids. I watched how all the violence really began with those two drugs. Back in the late sixties and early seventies boats would pull right up in Lynn Harbor (like many of the surrounding towns) and unload huge bails of drugs. The bails would then be loaded onto moving trucks and they would disappear down the road, with a State Trooper giving them an escort. It truly was a different time.

After two friends from New York and I were ganged up on (known as being rat packed) by a biker club based out of Detroit with a Boston chapter, something changed inside me forever. I came to, the next day, three towns over and face down in the mud, all busted up and the only thing I could move without pain was one eye.

I made a decision within myself in that moment that I would never be the one left on the ground again. I would not hesitate to use a gun, knife, car, truck, or any other weapon, in the blink of an eye. I became willing to go all the way, to take a life if necessary, without any hesitation.

I made a decision within myself that day that changed me and changed the way people were to treat me. I was to experience a new respect from people. In a primitive, warrior society, it would be called the passage or rites into manhood. A decision will change you into a whole different person and people will sense it. It is a very powerful tool. I was to gain a new respect from people, without having to do anything or even say anything. They could just tell, that I had an unshakable conviction about myself that they could feel. The vibration that I put out was a calm but completely confident energy regarding myself. They knew my days of taking any shit from anyone, were over. I must admit that I love having made that decision.

That decision took me from feeling like a helpless victim to giving me such a feeling of power. I have never been afraid of anyone ever again. Seeing the power of a gun very young also showed me that anyone, not matter how big, can be dropped in a heartbeat. Knowing it does not take much to end the existence of something that is made of only flesh and blood. The life of a Human being is really pretty fragile and it is only the ego that makes men think they are supermen. A person's title, uniform, gang colors, position in society never meant anything to me and it still doesn't. Some of the greatest people have no title and some of the worst people are world leaders. It is all about who the person truly is.

I am grateful that today I live in a world where having to take actions like that, are unnecessary. When you finally know that you create the world you live in and that you draw only the people that you expect to be in your life to you. You will create a world of peace and happiness. I know my life is in God's hands.

So as not to bore you with a lot of the same kind of stuff, this last story should give you an overall look at those years. Thankfully, they are over. At nineteen years old, I followed my brother Skip into the 12-step program and began my spiritual recovery from a fatal illness. I was to experience a lot over those years that followed and will be eternally grateful for the program. After getting sober, I returned to work in the Teamsters Union. Through my uncle a Teamster Boss (a friend of Jimmy Hoffa), I had worked around the union since I was fifteen years old. And then joined legally at eighteen years old. I loved driving the big rigs and I was very fortunate to have a career that I loved. Because of my anger, I would last only a couple of years on any particular job and then my uncle would put me on another job with a different type of truck. So out of my character defect of being so angry, I ended up driving every type of truck or piece of equipment that the Teamsters are responsible for. I became the driver that they could send to any of these difficult jobs, because of my driving experience. They would put me on these jobs as the union steward.

Once again in my life, a seemingly bad thing of having a violent temper turned out to be a great benefit in my life. I eventually worked in the construction division of the Teamsters Union and drove all the oversized rigs, 50 to 85-ton earthmovers, cat wagons, swivel dumps, oversized tractor-trailers and double trailers. I worked a lot of the time in Boston. I loved working with the construction unions and around the piers of Boston and meeting and becoming friends with some of the wise guys that were involved in Boston's organized crime. Some of them would take jobs in the unions, as a cover for their involvement in criminal affairs. It is interesting to have met so many people from different walks of life and to see that there is good and bad in every person and that people basically are all the same. I have always had an addiction to danger and excitement and I am lucky to be in one piece and still above ground.

On a lighter note, here are some pictures of me back in the early days. I have now been riding for over fifty years, since 1965, and back in the late sixties and early seventies, some of the pictures of me riding wheelies and riding my Harley down the street standing on the seat with my arms stretched out, made it into a California Motorcycle magazine. So, there is hope, you can also have your 'five minutes of fame'.

That was me on my shovelhead

A guy named Cal, who was from California, was riding alongside me. We were both standing on the seats of our Harleys, with our arms stretched out, blasting through the streets of Lynn, until he fell off and broke both his ankles. Back in the early seventies, I flipped my bike over backwards while riding a wheelie and slid for about forty feet in front of the Iron Works, a very hard-core motorcycle shop owned by Dickey Ski and Jimmie T. They named me the wheelie king.

That was my second five minutes of fame. I left the hospital on the back of another Harley, all bandaged up and with crutches in hand. Junior, who was driving the Harley that I was riding on the back of, proceeded to ride a wheelie in front of the hospital. They say there is something in the drinking water down in Lynn that just makes everyone crazy.

You probably don't see this everyday. I also did wheelies with other vehicles, like this 50-ton earthmover. A 50-ton wheelie, now that's pretty cool. I had gotten married and had a son, Benjamin and a daughter, Rachel and eventually moved to Maine to live. It was another seven-year period of my life. I feel the real purpose of the marriage was to bring these two souls into the world. It was so well worth it. As anyone who has children knows, having a child is the most incredible experience in this life. It was for me anyway. It was a pretty painful marriage for everyone involved, but I know in my heart it was all meant to be and I am so grateful for Benjamin and Rachel. And now my daughter Rachel has given us the gift of Shayla, my granddaughter.

Shayla and Barbara, Girl Riders.

After many years in the 12-step program, my brother Skip started practicing an ancient yogic practice, also known as Kundalini Yoga. It is basically meditation that has been practiced and passed down for thousands of years. I was around twenty-five years sober when Skip sent me a book by a meditation Master. Now I had not opened a book, since the seventh grade in Catholic school, but this book was to change my life. It was the initiation into this new level of spiritual growth. They say not to go by appearances but to go by your own experience and mine was that by just reading this information, it was changing my life. I was literally experiencing something, that I had never experienced from anything else in this world. I was to experience the most awesome power from these teachings. They say that we are a part of God, so God's powers are our powers. These teachings are so powerful they opened my mind and heart to a new expansion beyond my wildest imagination. The gift of Yoga, Self-knowledge, just keeps giving.

Also, something that was such a powerful experience in my life was of making 'decisions', as I have written elsewhere in the story. Making a decision to go all the way with whatever you are involved with, will literally give you a new feeling of power and self-respect. Year's back, I had made a decision, to go all the way, with the 12-step program. It caused amazing changes and the inner doors of the program opened for me. All the secrets that had eluded me were revealed. Making a decision is a very powerful experience and affects everything in your life. Well, this will give you an idea of where I came from and it tells you a little bit about the early years.

This is a picture of Peter and his 120 Pro Street Racer.
'Don't you think I look like your average Yogi?'

Mysticism in Newburyport

Newburyport is a small coastal city in Essex County, Massachusetts. It is thirty-five miles northeast of Boston, and similar in many ways to Salem, another historic seaport and Gloucester, which also has a fascinating maritime history. The rich history of this unique little town is pretty amazing. Newburyport was the smallest town in Massachusetts when approved by the Governor Francis Bernard on February 4, 1764. This town reminds you of the pictures you see in history books, of early settlements along the river, where the people's life's flourished because of the easy access to the Atlantic Ocean. This easy access gave them great mobility for travel and commerce.

Newburyport's location is unique as the downtown is right on the Merrimac River, with such a short distance to the Atlantic Ocean. Where the Merrimac River and the Ocean meet, you will find some of the most treacherous currents. One side of the mouth of the river is Plum Island, beachfront properties and miles of preservation land, which continues into Ipswich and all the way down to Gloucester. The other side of the river's mouth is the Salisbury Reservation. The Reservation runs all along the banks of the river and on the ocean side you will find long stretches of magnificent beaches, going all the way into New Hampshire and Maine. The coastline from Salisbury, Mass., continues to Portsmouth Harbor, Kittery Point, York Harbor, Ogunquit Beach and then Wells Harbor.

The grand homes of the sea captains, with their widow walks, along High Street were like huge mansions and were staffed with African and Native American slaves at the time, which seems hard to believe when you visit this wonderful little town. William Lloyd Garrison, who most people have heard of, was born in Newburyport and he was responsible for the abolitionist movement reaching a peak with their Underground Railroad activities. For the record, Newburyport had never been comfortable with slavery and because of that, abolitionism took a firm hold in the town.

Newburyport once had a fishing fleet that operated from Georges Bank to the mouth of the Merrimack River. It also was a center for privateering during the Revolutionary war and the war of 1812. Beginning about 1832, it added numerous ships to the whaling fleet and also flourished with what was called the triangular trade, importing West Indian molasses and exporting rum made from the local distilleries located around Market Square. Market Square is the heart of this tale and you can feel its rich seafaring past surrounding you everywhere in this unique town. There were gun manufacturers and numerous ship builders and just a bustling maritime seaport, steeped in history, which you will experience with just a simple walk through town. Today, the town is a mix of little shops, full of tourists and boaters, almost exclusively recreational ones from all over the world, and it is a totally different place from those olden days. But you can still feel the heritage in the atmosphere with the smell of the river and the ocean. You will know its history in every breath of its air, truly a nice safe place to visit and call home. As I said, lots of history here: The first United States Coast Guard Station; first of many subsequent clipper ships built here; first 'Tea Party' rebellion to oppose

British Tea Tax; first state mint and treasury building and Newburyport's Superior Courthouse was the oldest, continuously active courthouse in Massachusetts. And these are just some of the many historic facts of this little town. Another of the magnificent places in Newburyport is the Maudslay State Park. This park was formerly the Moseley family estate, with walking, biking and horse trails and 19-century spectacular gardens. Along with the great energy of the river and the ocean, you also have all kinds of wildlife, nature preserves and just an abundance of life, health, happiness and people loving the life they live. There is a closed off area in Maudslay State Park that is a special nesting place for the Bald Eagles. These magnificent birds spend the winter in the park and fish the Merrimac River. That river is the heart of this book of tales.

In recent days, this powerful energy center has also drawn many spiritual minded and gifted people to come to live here. There is a multitude of talented, evolved, creative, generous, supportive, very rare individuals making this area truly a one of a kind place to live and thrive. And Victoria's Secret has one of their main offices in downtown Newburyport. How great is that? People like the WWE superstar and movie star John Cena, a local guy that has become a household name around the world, because of his great heart. John is one of the most authentic, down-to-earth people you could ever meet. John has granted more than 500 wishes for the 'Make a Wish Foundation', more than anyone else. Having had the opportunity to get to know John and his brothers from the Hard Nock's Gym, I have to say that my respect for John is much more than his physical successes, which are absolutely amazing. It is really for the person, he is humble, grateful and always quick to lend a hand. John is truly a rare, authentic man and it is a privilege to know him. John has always honored and has never forgotten those who have played a part in his success and in his life. Dave Nock, for one, comes to mind. I mentioned to John that I was writing a book and that one of the stories was about the Hard Nock's Gym and would he mind if I mentioned him in the story. He said; "Sure." John always comes across as generous and sincere and I know that is why he is so well liked and respected.

Another of the extremely creative and very successful locals is a man named Jay Schadler, a two-time Emmy Award winning journalist and photographer. He has worked out of New York City on many fascinating projects. He also maintains a studio, high in one of the local buildings around the Newburyport area that looks like something you would see in the high-end district in LA or New York City. It is filled with amazing creations. Jay was another one of these great people that I had the privilege to meet. He also said he would be happy to let me use one of his pictures in my book; another generous, successful and authentic great person from this area.

A sweetheart of a woman from the Newburyport area, that truly touched my heart with her sincerity and wisdom was, Cheryl Richardson. Cheryl was to become one of the most influential figures in the realm of self-help and natural healing. She is one of the Hay House International authors and when Louise Hay transitioned from her body, Cheryl left one of the most moving tributes on YouTube. When you come across a woman like Cheryl or Louise that are so unconditionally loving, sincere, kind, genuine, generous and helpful, it just melts your heart. This experience of having your heart touched in such a positive way goes so far beyond all the day-to-day meaningless stuff we all can get caught up in. Rev. Shipley from Unity on the River church and Cheryl shared a great friendship and common love of service. These two women have played a part for many more people than they might ever realize, me included. Those are the kind of people that live around here and some of the reasons that this area is so alive with positive energy.

One of the gathering places for these great people is Unity on the River, a church of celebration, which is one of the most spirit-filled places I have ever had the privilege to attend. It is a place that supports and respects whatever path you are on to find the God of your understanding. The pastor, a beautiful and gifted woman whose name is Shipley, guided the church from its conception many years ago. The Church had it's beginning in the basement of the bank in Newburyport. And the church has flourished with a congregation of very evolved people. It is one of the most spirit-full and unconditional loving places I have ever been since starting this journey.

Another place that played such a huge part for me was called Hard Nocks Gym, the oldest running gym in this area since 1960 and where John Cena started his training. This gym has the most standup group of guys and gals I have ever met, amazing physical strength, focus, dedication, supportiveness, fair mindedness and just great people. They are people like John and Jay, who are authentic great individuals. In this world today, people who are honest, sincere, kind and generous are rare to find, and this area around here is full of these types of people living their lives fully and making the most of the present moment. It was a first for me to share this kind of fellowship, without having to show your loyalty by hurting any outsiders. These are just a few of the people and groups around Newburyport giving you an idea of the perfect atmosphere I had arrived in, to complete a huge piece of my karma.

When I arrived in Newburyport, I was instantly drawn to the river and felt a palpable magnetic pull. I was not sure what that pull was, as so much started happening for me at that time, including powerful influences from my past. It turned out that it was the time for me to come to terms with past actions and pay the price for my destructive behaviors. No one gets away with anything in this life and we truly get back what we have given, with exact mathematical precision. I was being bombarded with what appeared to be 'seemingly' past lives. All these things started happening, right after I started reading a book by a meditation master.

I was to learn later that right in the heart of Market Square is one of the earth's magnetic and spiritual crossroads. Gregg Braden, spiritual teacher and scientist, mentioned that the research of leading scientists are finding the convergence of three powerful cycles of nature coming together and creating what the scientists call "a time of extremes," at this time in our history. The first 'extreme' is of climate cycle change, the second is of an economic cycle and the third is a cycle of conflict. Scientists feel that this could be a first-time experience in the history of the planet that all these three cycles have come together at one time. Interesting that once again modern science is on the same page with the ancient teachings as found in the yogic traditions. These traditions talk of the present time that we are living in as the darkest of all ages, calling it Kali Yuga.

Ancient civilizations believed that the body of our physical blue planet materialized from a universal energy matrix and has a subtle structure, similar to the human energy field. As in the physical body, we have seven energy centers called chakras. These ancient civilizations believed that the Earth has seven major chakras. Also, energy vortexes located on each continent. These civilizations built sacred monuments in these areas such as Stonehenge, the Pyramids of Egypt and Mayan, sites of the Aztec and Incan civilizations and all were holy pilgrimage sites.

Mt. Shasta in California is one site that is believed to be the root chakra, which runs like a dragon from Northern California through Oregon, Washington and to the Canadian border. If Mt. Shasta is the tail of the dragon, then Mt. Rainier is its mouth, or head. The other Earth chakras are believed to be Lake Titicaca; the Solar Plexus chakra, Uluru-Katatjuta, Australia, that massive rock formerly known as Ayers Rock; the heart chakra, Glastonbury and Shaftsbury, England; the throat chakra, Great Pyramid of Giza; the third eye, Kuh-e Malek Siah, triple border of Iran, Afghanistan and Pakistan and of course Mt Kailas, Tibet, would be the crown chakra. Something that happens, once you start on this path, is seeing there is just one story.

Another example of just one story is, as in our body we have a spine and chakras or energy spots. So, too, does the Earth with its spine, the mountain ranges and these earthly chakras. Writing this book has been the best gift to myself, as it has brought everything together for me and given me clarity and complete validation, about my true purpose and my personal path. With the passing of Louise Hay, Wayne Dyer and others, I have decided (in my own small way) that my life's purpose is to try and keep passing on these priceless gifts that I have received from these wonderful people to anyone receptive.

Amazingly enough, the scientists also identify places with the opposite negative reactions, called 'vile vortexes' or 'electromagnetic disturbances', such as the Bermuda Triangle and the Devil's Sea, east of Japan. The fluctuations in the electromagnetic field causes problems with radar and other electronics and is probably the cause of many of the missing ships and aircrafts. One other place that is a powerful crossroads for these earthly energies is Sedona, Arizona and another one closer to home is Market Square, Newburyport, Massachusetts. Layne, an amazing woman from the area, was a master of being able to detect these types of places. She also was involved in some group, out in Sedona, doing this advanced exploration. I was to experience for myself what she had discovered in this area. I was to find it right here in the middle of town, which was a crossroads of this magnetic Earth's pathway. As I sat in Market Square one night after a long meditation, I realized that the four points of the geographic locations that these tales were written about came together right where I was sitting. I was sitting in the dead center of them.

The river was to the North, and Old Hill Burial Grounds was to the South. The Atlantic Ocean was to the East and Pow Wow Hill, the ancient Native American burial grounds, was to the West. I was sitting smack dab in the middle of the vortex of North, South, East and West converging, right in Market Square. The Square is a place where the energy convergence is physically palpable, if you are only open to it. It explains why it has been a gathering place for many, many years for the inhabitants of this area.

Market Square is the heart of Newburyport and magnetically draws people to it, whether they are consciously aware of that or not. Gregg Braden mentioned in one of his talks how we have been monitoring the earth's electro-magnetic levels by satellites and how there was a huge spike in these levels on 9/11. The scientific data of today proves that human emotion actually 'affects the physical world we live in' and that we are not separate from the Earth, but we are all connected. This truly is a living planet, as shown in the past. The Earth has literally made adjustments in itself to maintain its temperature, so as to sustain life here, as we know it. It truly is a living planet and we are a part of this Earth, made up of the same elements. The best scientists of the past said that human beings and the Earth were not connected. We know now that the Earth and human beings are not only connected, but originate from the same Source. So, we are completely connected and we can actually affect our world around us, through our thoughts, feelings and emotions. Now, if you are into power, *this is true power*. We all are like little Gods creating our life and our worlds, in every moment and though our thoughts. Thought is the only creator. *God is simply a law of cause and effect* and our thoughts are the cause of everything. So, what are you waiting for? Create something worthwhile for yourself. What could be more exciting than learning about yourself and this world, as this world and you are your life?

I became fascinated with the latest knowledge of Quantum Science, which tells us that the emotions in our hearts can actually change our DNA and change the Atoms in us and around us, so giving us complete power and control of our health and life. The Heart Math Institute in California is doing amazing work in this new field of science and healing. If you take nothing else from this book, take some time and learn about the most powerful, creative device in the entire universe and that it is your Own Mind and your Own Heart, which are not separate. When the monks chant and meditate for hours, what they are doing is creating a feeling within themselves and *the feeling is the prayer*. This is key, to creating your dreams, as this feeling/prayer is the fuel that will bring your visualization into the physical world. The ancient Masters have told in detail exactly how to create these miracles and now the Western scientists are proving that it is all true through their research. Not that you would ever need validation, after experiencing this power for yourself.

During the time, I wrote the tale called "Tidemaster" all of these questions were answered for me through meditation, reading powerful information and time in the silence. In a sense, all these truths are hidden in plain sight from most people. You need the key of an open mind to enter this realm of wisdom. The river was also such a powerful influence in the writing of these tales and in my life. The river called and I answered, by returning back to the river and back to what feels like my home. The river feels like it has been my home for many, many lifetimes. When these experiences started happening along the river, my great friend Jeff Smith gave me a copy of the book called *Siddhartha*, by Hermann Hesse and I was blown away. It described what was happening to me along the banks of this river. In this book, the boatman named Vasudev tells Siddhartha to stay by the river and "the river will tell you everything." And that was to be true for me also. It is just one of the many ways Nature teaches you all about life. Communion with Nature is such a priceless gift that we all can share. Every time you walk into Nature you are reuniting with God.

Around the same time, on one of my visits to an ashram, I got to meet the mediation Master and I asked for a spiritual name. The Swami who was my intermediate with the meditation master had the same name as the boatman that I had come to love in the novel called *Siddhartha*. The names being the same, at the same time I was having these experiences, is just another of the many coincidences at that time. The name given to me that night was Kushala. The kusha grass was considered worthless, until the monks started weaving it together for their meditation mats and from then on it was revered.

Today everyone is familiar with the benefits of yoga and meditation and how much it does for your health, mind, body, and soul, but then there is another kind of *MEDITATION*, an ancient science. This special type of meditation is empowered from true lineages of meditation Masters that goes back to the beginnings of time in an unbroken lineage. Can you imagine people focusing and practicing on one thing for five or six thousand, maybe ten thousand years, how powerful that would be? I came across one of these authentic paths and my life has literally increased a thousand fold, in every area, since my using these simple practices of meditation, time in the silence, contemplation and communing with Nature. These practices bear fruit in so many ways. In meditation, I would remember things that had long been forgotten. Some were experiences with my father and some with friends. In a guided meditation it talked of how your emotions will become like a still pond. My mind went back to a time of being a very young child and I was with my father in Marblehead, Massachusetts. I was sitting on the edge of a pond with a toy boat my father had gotten me. In the meditation I experienced being right there once again. I had the best father. In the meditation it talked about how *your mind will become like a lamp set in a windless place*. I just love that one.

In one of my meditations, I flashed back to the early seventies and remembered a conversation with my friend Buster. Buster had mentioned how he was making another trip to Europe and the Scandinavian countries, as he was on the 'Approval Committee' for accepting riding clubs that wanted to become chapters of the riding club from America. I truly had some powerful friends in the motorcycle world in the old days. Well, back to the story, I went from living a life of settling for crumbs to a life of health and success in everything I did. Living with wealth in all areas of life, with incredible people and fulfilling relationships, abundance and prosperity in all aspects of my life.

But the best gifts were of the ability to know how to live, how to think correctly, how to create anything I want, and how to breathe. Breathing is a science in itself. And, also learning what life is truly all about for me and to never feel alone or incomplete again. When through grace and your willingness to be open to this force, which has always been right under our noses, this divine power (God) will introduce itself to you, in your mind, heart, body and soul, which has just been waiting there to be unfolded. And you will explode with bliss, beyond anything you could have ever imagined. You will go from a limited world/life view to an infinite, expanded view of seeing a whole new world and universe and a knowing that all possibilities are readily available to you, 'just for the asking'.

I could fill a whole book on the quotes that have revolutionized my thinking and my life and that book may be one that I write down the road. I have more than seventy notebooks of heart-touching quotes from Masters and Spiritual Teachers. Their words can reach deep inside you and touch you in a way that goes beyond your mind and senses. So many of us live by our five senses, which gives us access to about five % of what is going on in the overall picture of this world. And we foolishly believe that we know the whole story. One of the interesting things that happens the more you see and know, is that instead of this knowledge going to your head and thinking how wise you are. You have a feeling of deep humility and gratitude for the universe revealing itself to you. You know you are but a grain of sand on the beach. It actually has a very humbling effect on you and all the while you appear to others to be someone very powerful, because of this awakened force within you. With me being someone with only a seventh-grade formal education to try and put my experiences into words it could easily fall short of being clearly communicated. But once again, it is always about the intention and vibration, so lack of formal education means little in the real world. Also, because of our connection with the Universal Mind, through our own subconscious mind, we have access to unlimited knowledge and wisdom. It is available for everyone because it is the sleeping giant right within you.

So, the story really begins for me returning to the river and being surrounded in this richly filled land of energetic, spiritual people along with the rich history of the sea. The influence and wisdom of the Native American culture, an incredible connection with nature and also with the spiritual energy exploding within me from these ancient teachings of the science of mind, breath and consciousness, everything began to unfold for the adventure of a lifetime. It was like the perfect storm when these forces came into play with my returning to the river. I believe the River pulled me right to it when the time was right. The energy of this Newburyport area can easily be related to by the example that if you went into a prison, no one has to tell you that you are in a prison; you can feel a real heavy and negative presence right in the air that surrounds you. It's hard to even breathe. Likewise, you can equally feel a powerful positive uplifting energy in places where seekers have done spiritual practices for many years. You will feel the Presence as a real force and if you are fortunate enough to go to a place like that, you will be drawn right into a deep meditation. The river is part of Nature and Nature is God. And the Intelligence behind Nature (God) is in every cell of our bodies. I do mention this truth many times in these stories. When people are in Nature they may not know what they are feeling, but they know they are experiencing something. They have returned to their source and are once again re-joined with God.

At the time, I was making numerous trips, to upstate New York, where the ashram of a meditation Master from India was located. I would return from these trips so full, with this unexplainable energy. I was just soaring and miracles were happening on a daily basis. This energy had taken me to a place where I was to experience things way above any of my abilities. I started swimming every day that summer and I decided that I would stop if and when I got cold. Well, I walked into the ocean at least a couple days every month that year, right through the winter and never was cold, completely unaffected by the winter temperature. In the spring, I mentioned it to someone, 'maybe a little bragging' and then the next time I put my foot into the ocean water, I thought my toes were going to freeze and drop off. God had given me a gift and it was meant for me and not to be used to puff up my ego. God also has a great sense of humor. God is happiness, love, joy, laughter, humor and lightheartedness. When I am lighthearted, I am coming from spirit (God) and when I am very serious, I am coming from ego.

As I sat in meditation on the banks on the Salisbury side of the river, at a place called Butler's Toothpick, a wooden pyramid structure used as a reference by the sailors. I had a realization. I saw how to swim the mouth of the river, with its treacherous currents and it seemed like it could so easily be accomplished. A statement that I use with my friend Sandi, when she is caught up in stuff that is just wasting her time is, "Don't you have anything better to have your mind on?" I am sure people could have used that statement regarding me, with me having my mind on swimming the mouth of this river. But, I was smart enough not to tell anyone. I may be Irish, but I am not stupid.

First I had to wait until the end of the season, so all the recreational boats were out of the water, eliminating a lot of traffic and only leaving an occasional fishing boat. It takes most of the summer to warm the vast waters of the ocean, but the other side of that is that it takes time for the ocean to get cold again, so swimming in the fall is no problem, especially with the temporary gift I had received of being unaffected by the water's temperature. On the Salisbury side of the river are these collections of rocks and when the tide goes out and flows over them, it sounds like the turbines at the General Electric Plant. The rocks and tide would tear you to shreds if you did not time your swim exactly. So the real trick is situating yourself out on the rocks about a hundred feet off shore, at just the right time, during the ebb tide, the temporary stillness of the tides. Then from there you would swim as fast as you can straight across into the river. The sandbar on the opposite side on Plum Island extends way over, almost to the Salisbury side, so if you could swim far enough into the river before the tide starts back out, you could let the tide do the work. Just like the philosophy taught in *The Art of War*. And it will put you up on the other side and onto Plum Island. It would be a piece of cake. Of course, if your timing was wrong, the next stop would be Portugal. The only scary part is getting positioned on the rocks, as the harbor seals cover the rocks and can be pretty territorial. You would not want to tangle with them in the water on their turf.

So the boating season came to an end and I made my first attempt. I made it to the rocks with no problem, even from the local inhabitants, the harbor seals. I waited for just the right time and started swimming straight across the river. I had watched the Coast Guard patrols and knew their schedules, but on this day they did not play fair and they were to change up their practical routines. They came up the river and ruined my first attempt to complete my swim. My next two attempts turned out similar, as I had to turn back due to fishing boats. Because of the length of time it took for me to swim far enough into the river, there always seemed unwanted company showing up. So I decided to wait longer into the year and that was when Barbara entered my life and my simple life of meditation and spending all my time in solitude and nature changed dramatically. I am not complaining, as I was to have an equally wonderful next ten years with Barbara. I was to learn so much from this gifted woman. So I let that adventure die a natural death. Maybe, God knew the results of my swimming the mouth of the river would not be as I saw it unfolding. Also my being unaffected by cold was also gone now, which made the swim without a wetsuit impossible. I considered wearing a wetsuit would be cheating, so it was on to better things.

The Newburyport area and the river has that kind of powerful unexplained spiritual presence that you read about in books and I believe it is due to the connection with nature, which is God, and along with the people's appreciation and love of living here along the river, and with this ocean of abundance of life bursting in this area. They say that God loves gratitude and will bestow grateful people with even more blessings. Although many may not know why they love being there, they do know it is a place dear to their hearts, as it is to my own heart. In these stories, I will relate the best I can, and the most accurately and truthfully as I can, what was to transpire in the following years. Most of what happened at this time was really beyond my comprehension with my limited understanding and knowledge. I had to rely completely on the recorded history of these meditation Masters.

Each reader will come to their own conclusion about these tales and that is the way it will be. If you can try not to judge them, but see if there is something of use in these tales for you, that would be a great gift to me. These experiences rocketed me into vast inner worlds and higher realms of consciousness and eventually gave me an unshakeable conviction of my divinity. That conviction was that the wisdom told by the Masters from thousands of years ago, of the undeniable truths of existence, 'is the absolute truth'. Sometimes you can see or hear about a person who is so filled with enthusiasm for life, completely carefree and lighthearted and your mind just cannot understand how this is possible. We all have that enthusiasm inside ourselves and sometime, somewhere, everyone will have his or her day in the Sun. In the beginning years of these experiences, I was reluctant to share what was happening inside me. I was not sure if I had not finally gone over the deep end, but I did not care, as I had never felt so good. I was experiencing things that I had only heard about and probably laughed at in the past, experiences like the blind seeing and the deaf hearing and being filled with the spirit of God. I had witnessed my great friend, Big Ben being filled with this spirit of God. But now it was 'my time' to experience these gifts and it all began to make perfect sense.

I was someone who had arrested his alcoholism and had recovered from that disease and had attained all that the program of recovery had to offer, including the promises of health, happiness, prosperity, peace of mind, knowing how to live, and emotional sobriety. But my heart had never fully opened to the Love that resided deep in my own heart. That was to happen shortly after returning home to the river and my reawakening. One of the first examples of how this was all unfolding for me was when I would look across the river from the boardwalk to the opposite shore, where there was a four-story house, with windows facing the river.

There would be nights, interestingly, it would coincide with the level of my spiritual energy, that every window (the eyes of the house) would have golden light pouring out from the heart of the house. It seemed alive. The house would just light up the river. In the same way the physical body (the vehicle for the soul) would pour out the love of God through the sparkling eyes of the uplifted individual. A person's eyes can tell you the whole story of their life. I started being able to look right into someone's eyes and go deep inside them and know all their deepest secrets and desires. As if they had become an open book for me to read. Somehow this was happening by just looking in their eyes, because the eyes are the 'gateway to a person's soul'.

The best way I can relate these experiences of having connected to this awesome power of God is by using this simple example of me at the computer. When I sit at the computer, 'not online', it's just me with my limited abilities, but when I plug into the Wi-Fi, I connect worldwide with unlimited information about anything and everything. So, that's also true about myself, with the limited capabilities of my conscious mind and ego. Then, through grace, I'm able to get out of my own way and connect with Universal Consciousness, through the subconscious mind. I then connect with unlimited powers, the powers of God, which are beyond my wildest imagination and which give me a knowing that I have access to all possibilities and full potential in every aspect of life. I can be anything I want to be, I can have anything I want and I can do and accomplish everything my heart truly desires. My capabilities have no limit anymore.

The amazing thing about this principle is that 'what you think will be true for you'. If you believe that your capabilities are unlimited then they will be unlimited. If you believe you are powerless, a victim of life and have very limited abilities that will be true for you. That is why understanding the power of your own mind and your heart is so important. Your heart is actually the most powerful magnetic force in your body, even greater than your brain.

One night, as I minimized a picture from the screen of my computer and watched it all be drawn down to a little icon and then I hit maximize and from the little icon, the whole screen filled with the picture, once again, it reminded me of how 'Out of God everything and everyone flows' and becomes this life and this world, and then God experiences himself or herself, and then one day draws it all back into it's own being, so nothing really happened, except the Play of God or the Play of Consciousness. All the religions, true spiritual paths, and latest scientific research tell us *it is all coming from one intelligent source.* As the spider weaves its web out of itself and then one day draws all of it back into itself, it is the easiest example I can give for how God works. As I sit here tonight, I remember a story I heard forty-seven years ago when I entered the 12-step program and it goes like this: The young boy was bothering his father, who had work he had to finish, so his father tore up this map of the world and told the son, when you can put the map back together, I will play with you. So the young boy left for a very short time and came back with the map all put together. The father was shocked and asked how did he do it so quickly. The boy said that on the back of the map was a picture of a man and when I put the man together 'all of the world just fell into place'.

When you truly know who you are, you will live fearlessly in a whole new, different world. That world will be a world of health, happiness, prosperity and unconditional love and it is here for anyone. I choose to live in God's world and God's world is a world of love, abundance, prosperity, health and happiness for anyone who will open their mind and heart to what is 'already within our own hearts'. That is actually our natural state. It is a state of peace, love and harmony, before the ego and mind complicate everything with all the rights and wrongs, shoulds and have to's, good and bad, seeing things either black or white, with all the manmade rules. These are words that will fall from your vocabulary, along the way. Then it truly is a journey to return to the innocence of a child, being lighthearted and carefree.

So, I began enjoying this wonderful little town and I started reading books, mostly from the Far East, and D. R. Butler's correspondence course. I had not read a book since the seventh grade, when I left the Catholic school system. I went into public schools and never opened another book and was passed on each year by just showing up enough days for what they called Social Promoting, which started in the late sixties. I basically learned nothing. Within the next few years, after reading my first yogic book, I was to read more than 200 books. I was devouring them and could not get enough. My thirst could not be quenched, being an Irish alcoholic and an addict for more… more… more. That unquenchable thirst for whatever I was into just came naturally to me. I became an avid reader and it all was easily understandable for me, even the advanced teachings. I do believe that people are just remembering teachings that they already know from spiritual practices performed in their past lives.

I see this in my granddaughter Shayla's eyes all the time. She is an old soul that has come back to keep me in line and to share great love. Shayla has so touched the heart of this old pirate. One of the teachings was that you will manifest as 'you believe yourself to be' and I had always believed I was not book smart so I appeared as someone who was not very well educated. At the time, I had a chance to go to school for a year full time, paid by the union and I took it. I was told I would have to take a reading test. I thought, *I can't be bothered with this nonsense* and when she gave me the test I just blasted through it and turned it in.

In a few days she called and said that she had some good news and some bad news. The bad news was that because I have no formal education they were going to test me at a lower reading level, but they made a mistake and gave me the advanced reading test. She said, "The good news is that you got a perfect score." So the truth was that I was actually very intelligent, scoring high in what they call 'emotional intelligence', but because my belief was that I was not very smart, that had become my reality for most of my life. Wow, what an example of 'What you think is what you get'.

I had found many great places to do my meditation practices and my reading all around the area and started having very interesting insights and experiences. When you start on the spiritual journey you think it is going to be all cake and ice cream and it actually turns out to be a complete rearranging of you and your life and a purging of all your negative baggage. You'd best plan on hanging on by your fingertips. I just realized that's why most people don't want to hear about it. Sometimes in meditation, I would have wonderful feelings and memories and then at other times I would remember some very painful times and really have to fully witness them for the first time.

One of the first memories that came back was of being the last one to be with my friend Ritchie just before he died of multiple gunshot wounds. I had never even thought about or acknowledged that incident and after all these years I was re-experiencing that night like it was right here and now. I was to learn that a spiritual awakening on a true spiritual path is not the way it is portrayed in the movies. It actually is 'going to the big leagues'. It is all about coming face to face with the best about youself and the worst. At least this is how it has been for me. Every day we have lots of experiences, but we are so busy we process very few of them. Day after day all these unresolved things just keep getting stored in the back of our minds. When you start meditating, these impressions start revealing themselves to you, to get expelled and a few past experiences of mine came up that would have been real game changers for my life.

One night as I was sitting along the river, really having a great meditation, feeling happy, joyous and free, I remembered the night in my first year of sobriety that I almost got shot. One of the local, long-time bikers had told me a long time ago, that the way to take the power away from someone who was pointing a gun at you is to 'run at the gun'. That made perfect sense to me, in my twisted mind, and I was to experience putting that philosophy into practical use first-hand for myself.

I was hanging out and a guy pulled up along side me in his car and pulled out a gun. I just automatically dove through the car window at him. The guys I was with pulled me out and he took off. The next day, in broad daylight, we pulled up at his home and got out of the truck, pulled out guns and kicked in his front door and went in after him. If he had been home that day, this book would probably have a completely, different title, something like *Mysticism in State Prison*. He left town and eventually it was forgotten, and I was busy with my newly self-created problems. That was just an average day for people living in Lynn, Mass. On any day, in the blink of an eye, your life could change tragically forever. Another clear recollection came back in meditation, of a situation that was happening around my father's house.

There was a punk in the neighborhood that was bothering the older people and women when no one was around and my father was not someone to put up with that. I was afraid he might get hurt. I thought about it and the decision was obvious and that was to eliminate the threat. I made my plan and then put together the perfect weapons for this particular task. I found the perfect place and waited for the punk. It all just came so natural for me, and I experienced such a calm and peaceful feeling as I waited for his arrival. It was almost like a meditative state. At these times, I felt like another person, someone with the skills of an experienced assassin. I would just slide into this calm, emotionless state of being, with no conscience or guilt. I waited a long time and he did not keep to his usual routine, so I decided to take a ride and come back later that night. Something was to happen on that ride that changed my life for the better. This was my seventh year of sobriety and the year I finally got off the fence about joining a certain riding club. It was another seven-year cycle in my life. After two years of sobriety, my obsession for alcohol and drugs had been removed 'through grace' and I never have had that obsession again, except that fateful night. During my ride, I passed a liquor store and my mind started to torture me about going in and getting a bottle. The obsession for alcohol that God had removed five years earlier had returned. At the time, I really had no value of my own life or anyone else's, that's obvious, and I also did not care whether I got locked up. But there was one thing I did care about, above everything else in this world and that was my freedom from alcohol and drugs. When you are an active alcoholic you literally are a slave and have no say about anything and everyone is above you. My ego hated that. The next day I related my night to my sponsor, in the 12-step program, who had been locked up for many years for the same kind of behavior. He said that God removes the obsession to drink and did I think God, a loving God, would remove my obsession, when I was going around bumping people off? It made perfect sense and I knew any 'premeditated violence' was over. My sponsor laughed and said: "Most people don't have to take things this far to learn the lessons of the program. But because you have taken things this far on a number of occasions, you have knowledge and wisdom from going places most would never go."

There would be a few more spontaneous acts of this kind of behavior, but the grace of God would always intervene. My sponsor had said that I made the man upstairs, God, work overtime, and he also said the good part is that people will know you don't have to be a saint to be in a recovery program; that the hoop you jump through is bigger than you think. I can admit this stuff freely today because it has changed. But there had been a part of my personality that would show up and it was of an emotionless psycho, with no mercy or empathy for anyone, like I was dead inside, lacking any compassion. 'But for the grace of God', my life could have gone in a very different direction and I could have missed out on the best opportunity that anyone could ever have.

My destiny in this life was to end up living an exceptionally great life in peace and harmony, free from anger, rage and psychotic behavior. During this lifetime of mine, I believe I was to reap the rewards of many lifetimes of spiritual work and live as a free man, right here and now. Of course, God had to compensate for my human side, which was full of 'issues' and God has saved my ass a number of times, always giving me another chance. I finally saw my opportunity and I grabbed it and it has paid off richly. I considered removing these more negative bits of my experience, as someone had mentioned that they change the tone of the book, which is about returning to love. I thought about it and realized that life has many tones and that my story would be lost if I am not completely honest. And there is no one still alive that could testify against me anyway, so what the hell 'let's be honest'.

I never was the perfect little yogi type who never got a parking ticket. I was someone who lived a hell right within himself and some of that flowed out into the world. It is interesting, the misconception about a spiritual awakening and what happens when you begin on the spiritual path. You will have wonderful experiences and also all hell will break loose, all your demons and seemingly bad secret stuff will come to the surface and you will be forced to deal with it. When karma was explained to me, that you would get back exactly, what you have given or done to others, I was a little concerned, to say the least. One night Big Chris and I were walking from Hard Nock's Gym and a car came speeding around the corner and it seemed aimed right at us. Chris said: "Peter, you turned white as a ghost as it appeared that car was coming for us and then he said: Great, just because I am standing next to you, I am going to get killed because of some part of your karma." After a few deep breathes we both laughed. Chris has the same twisted sense of humor that I do.

Luckily, I was to learn that karma can actually be modified or changed, through spiritual practices and you really can escape some serious consequences. The path is truly about getting free of all your negative baggage and realizing that you are no better than anyone else. All good qualities and all bad qualities are in everyone to some degree. That truth gave me complete relief. I can remember hearing that a very evolved being said; that everyone has in them the same as what is in Mother Teresa and also everyone has in them the same as what was in Hitler. I did not like or understand that remark at the time, but since then I have come to see it as true.

In every human being are all possibilities. Star Wars was actually right, as we all have a dark side, besides the side of light. What happens is you start to see that you and everyone else are capable of great things and also are very capable of seemingly terrible things. And usually, before your life is over, you will have done a lot of both. It is just the human part of us and also a way God lets us experience being humbled, knowing we are not better than anyone else. Another thing that happens is you begin to see, almost like a silent witness, everything that is happening in your life 'is just another life experience', pretty meaningless, and not something to make into a big deal. I have always felt like someone completely detached and I was just witnessing this silly Irishman named Peter doing his thing, burning off his karma. I have felt like I was just playing different roles in movies and I never felt like the person I was portraying. That was all answered for me when I realized that my ego was not identifying with these temporary illusionary characters, which was a good thing.

I had the realization that it is the same one power that flows down my arms and into my hands to help someone or to hurt someone. It is all coming from one power Source. God has given us free will and it is up to us how we direct this unlimited power. *There is only one force, one power in this entire universe and we control and direct this power, through how we direct our thoughts.* People are like little Gods; everyday they are using God's power to create their lives through their thoughts and feelings into great lives or terrible lives. Or worse, just boring existences. And that is why, the knowledge of being responsible for ourselves is so important.

Well, lets get back to some of the more pleasant realizations and get out of the trenches of basic survival. Being infused with this energy from this spiritual path and its meditation Masters, my meditations came alive and were filled with amazing colors and images. I started to experience something that seemed like a movie camera projecting images outward, out one of my eyes, just the way a movie projector would project the images onto a screen. Our thoughts are like the movie projector and the world is the movie screen. The world is a mirror that reflects back to us what we are putting out. That changes everything; because we can create the images that get propelled out and become our life. We are responsible for every detail of our lives. Nothing happens that does not correspond to our predominant thoughts. So, there is nobody to blame anymore.

Something had happened inside me, an unexplainable force had been awakened and was causing experiences and insights and I was just in awe of this process. One of the greatest experiences I had at the time was after sitting in meditation for a long period of time, I saw with my mind's eye (or what my seven-year-old granddaughter Shayla informed me was also called the 'Third Eye'), a swirling blue light coming right at me, right between my eyes. It was like nothing I had ever seen before, so perfect, so smooth, so naturally flowing and it was the most beautiful shade of blue. I was to learn that it is called the Blue Pearl, the Self of the Universe. I was to start seeing this blue light around the street lamps and around car headlights.

The most interesting place I would see it was, as it appeared to be pouring out the side of the moon. I related it to when you have a tear in your coat and you can see the inner lining of the coat, the stuffing, and what the coat is really made of. This blue light is the Light of Consciousness, the light of the soul of the universe and it was pouring out the side of the moon, as if there was a tear in the lining of the universe and I was seeing the very image of God, the very heart of God. The scientists do call this 'the blue planet'. Some pictures of the Earth from space show this blue ring around the Earth.

I started having vivid pictures in my mind of nighttime drumming sessions around a blazing fire, under the bright moon and along the water's edge, with Native Americans, seemingly hundreds of years ago. I was to learn and experience that in consciousness, the past, present and future all exist right now and can be accessed through meditation practices.

Right around this time, I was to meet the 'Mystery Woman of Newburyport', with a chance meeting late at night on the boardwalk. The Newburyport boardwalk along the Merrimac River with a full moon is just spectacular. I had spent a long night sitting in the moonlight, which lit up the entire river and I was feeling such a connection with God and Nature. I had the place pretty much to myself, as my meditation had run late into the night. Somewhere in the middle of the night, I realized I was not alone, that just down the boardwalk from me was someone sitting as still as if they were part of the wooden structure. I was shocked, as I had been there for hours and had never noticed them, or even seen them move an inch. How could someone be so still for so long, out in a public place?

It would be a few nights later that I would see a woman on the boardwalk and I just knew it was the same person, even though I had not really got a good look at her on the past night. I just knew by her powerful presence. I said to her, "I believe we shared a moon together." She smiled and said: "Yes, so we did." Her name was Layne and she was to become my teacher of the river. Layne played the same part for me as the boatman named Vasudev did in the book *Siddhartha* and shared all the secrets of the river. She answered all my questions that had come up by my being in this area, and even my new purpose for the future. When I shared about this book of tales, she said with such conviction, "you need to be open to success with this book." You need to be open to the book going nationwide and even International. These words were so powerfully infused with energy that it actually seemed to change the way my life unfolded from that moment on.

Gregg Braden had mentioned that when you get an inner prompt to do something, that it was the universe telling you that there is something that someone needs and to follow your inner prompt. I feel that my purpose now is to share these wonderful gifts of this priceless knowledge with others. And share what I love and how I love to live today. If I help only one person on their journey, my life will be worthwhile. Layne completely understood everything I shared with her and said that is why she lived in this area, because of its powerful earthly energies, including the crossroads of these electromagnetic fields, and for the rich history of the people and Native American culture.

She also directed me to White Feather, an absolutely beautiful Native American healer, who has her own story later in the book and a place in my heart forever. They say that once you start on the spiritual path with all your heart, mind and soul everything you need for any goal will just start showing up. It has been true in my life and, once again, with this book. Everything and everyone I needed to edit, organize, publish and distribute came to me. How about this for a coincidence: My friend Bob, a retired college math professor who did the initial editing of this book, shared with me that his family goes back to 1698 in *Newburyport*. His ancestors go back to people that came over on the Mayflower. Really, where did I find this character? Miracles were starting to happen on a daily basis and the next seven-year cycle for me was another whirlwind and I just hung on for the ride. When you go from living in a small prison of a world and being very limited in your thought processes, to having astounding abilities through grace, you never will see yourself or the world the same. And it all is here for anyone who wants it.

It is said that you will initially receive seven physic powers, and they tell you not to get stuck there, for what is beyond is much greater. One example is of knowing the future; I thought to myself, *I have been seeing future events long before they happen. Are you kidding me? What could be greater than these powers?* Well, what is beyond them is much greater than the conscious mind can comprehend. And if we get stuck at this level of healer/visionary, with our ego identifying us as being a big deal because of these powers, we will stop the unfolding process of what lies at the highest level. You will be amused when you reach these higher levels and see what it actually is, but I will let you experience that for yourself.

Layne had an ability to detect these powerful electromagnetic places where the Earth's energy would cross, as an intersection does. Market Square in Newburyport is one of them. She has traveled all over the world, working for some mysterious group and was well known around the area. People would say that Layne had the ability to tell you something about yourself, some deep personal secret, that there was no way she could have known. Layne would just seem to appear out of nowhere and I was privileged to have had many talks with her. I am still in awe of this Mystery Woman. One of the places that I had experienced great energy in my meditations was Old Hill Burial Grounds. Depending on where it is written, it appears people call these burial grounds either Old Hill Burial or Old Burial Hill, so if you think you are misreading the name don't worry about it.

As Layne and I stood one night on the boardwalk, she said: "Put your hand on my heart." She placed one hand on my heart and her other hand over my hand on her heart and I did the same to her hand on my heart. Now we were standing on the boardwalk with people all around and she said: "Close your eyes and breathe in deeply. Now go back to before it was the graveyard." Almost instantly, I found myself high on Old Hill Burial Grounds with her, seemingly hundreds of years ago. And it felt like it was all happening right in that present moment. I had an immediate realization that she had been persecuted in the past for being so gifted. My legs buckled and actually right now it still gives me a cold shiver up my spine, like I am once again right there, right now, but at a time hundreds of years ago. And then she softly said to me, "You do remember don't you?" I muttered "Yes" in disbelief of whatever had just happened. I can see why women like her and her gifts could be mistaken for witches and witchcraft, as it is so far from what we know in the conscious realm. Layne is an amazingly powerful old soul in a beautiful woman's body. The entrance to Old Hill Burial Grounds has two pillars and on the plaque that is on one of these pillars says, "Seven of the crew of the Pocahontas are buried here." If you spend a night in meditation up there, maybe it will be your imagination, but you will feel like they still seem pretty active up on the hill in the moonlight. Imagine the energy of a graveyard full of sea captains, crewmembers, also possibly some of their slaves and a host of colorful characters from Old Newburyport. If it is true that we have an eternal soul and we really never die, who is to say that the feeling that you are not alone up on the hill is your imagination? After years of reading, studying and experiencing the information in Ram's course, including his first teacher's wisdom and the ancient teachings, I no longer have any doubt that all these inner worlds are nothing but the real deal and actually are 'the real world'. The inner world is eternal and this entire outer world is just temporary.

I have conviction and strength of who and what I am today, that I never even knew existed. People often will say they are afraid of this or that and it all seems perfectly acceptable to live in fear. But if you live in a 'fearless state', you are considered delusional. Really, which one sounds more desirable?

One night on the boardwalk Layne asked me, "Why the sadness?" I related that my daughter Rachel was struggling with some issues with herself (just like the rest of us go through). I felt helpless and did not know how to help her. Layne said, "A soul has come into this world and has not connected with the love, so she does not know if she wants to stay." She was once again so right and it was shortly afterward that things changed for Rachel. Her life today is full of love and purpose. One of the women who played a huge part for Rachel and Shayla was a woman named Nicky, a gifted healer from York, Maine, to whom I will be eternally grateful. Layne's comment explains why I had no value for my life until my heart opened and I experienced the love that is available for everyone.

I had wondered if I was meant to share more with Layne. When I asked her about that, she said she was to play a different part for me that she was not the one I would be with romantically. She said, "one day you will be with the woman you are meant to be with and that you will see me and I will smile at you." Some time passed and I had met Barbara and I knew instantly she was the one. One day as Barbara and I drove toward Barbara's home where I was now living, I saw Layne standing on a corner, on the outskirts of town. I looked up and she gave me this little smile and waved. I was speechless. Barbara asked me, what was that all about and I shared about the mystery woman, how I did not even know her last name or where she lived, even after years of sessions with her. I told Barbara about her prediction.

Barbara just smiled and waited a little while and then said, "Your Mystery Woman is now your next door neighbor." Their homes were in the most exclusive part of this area and literally sitting up high overlooking the river, *which is the heart of this book of tales.* Hmmm, that is another, interesting coincidence. Whatever Layne did to earn money, it paid her very well and she lived in elegance, befitting a queen.

Another bizarre incident was when I came across a book of photos of Newburyport contained the winning photographs from the area's photo contest. Jay Schadler had won a prize for his picture of the fountain behind the courthouse, with Old Hill Burial Ground in the background. That was the place I had many powerful meditations and also the very place that Layne and I had that seeming past-life flashback. A special area up on the hill, in front of one of the tombstones, was the place I was drawn to, and I did numerous long night meditations, on a bench set right in front of the stones.

In Jay's picture, there was a shaft of light coming down on and surrounding this very tombstone. I thought, *That is a pretty amazing picture,* I wondered whose name was on the stone. I went up to investigate.

The above is Jay's award-winning picture. I am grateful for his generosity, for allowing me to use this picture for my lighthearted book of tales.

The name on the stone was Benjamin, my son's name. My son had asked me, some year's back, not to call or try to contact him in any way. I thought it was kind of symbolic of where our relationship is at the present time and that in a sense our connection was dead to him. Hopefully, it is just a temporary situation. When Benjamin was born, it was one of the happiest and most touching moments of my life. The love I have for him has never changed and I can only wish him health, happiness and prosperity and wish him the best. I have not been the greatest person in this life and I can understand why someone might not want to be involved with me.

On a lighter note, I was to experience true happiness for the first time in my life with all the wonderful people and places in this area. And with the spiritual energy that had filled me to the brim. Many long nights out at the Salisbury Reservation in meditation and along the river, sometimes right through the entire night, feeling like I was in Heaven on Earth. I could have spent the rest of my life just meditating along the river and have been completely content. I could feel the life and energy of this amazing place and I would just dwell in the presence of God manifesting everywhere. God's eyes are the stars; God's voice is the pounding surf, the gurgling brook; God's bones are the mountains; God's arteries are the rivers and streams; God's breath is the wind. I never feel alone in Nature, as I feel I am truly home. And I would just savor my connection to God, through Nature. Somewhere along this journey, I was to see how completely I had been taken care of by a loving God and that everything had happened perfectly in my life to bring me to this moment. And now I can relive this precious moment over and over for the rest of my time while in this body. I know in my heart of hearts that I would not have arrived at this incredible place to live my life, if everything had not happened exactly as it did, including what seemed at the time to be bad experiences. This last year has been a time of huge changes and it has rocketed me into an even higher level of evolvement and accomplishment. I am experiencing an even better and greater existence while in this body.

I cannot express enough the life-changing benefits of just a few of the following ancient techniques. Some of them are; meditation, solitude, contemplation, the science of breath, writing stuff out, communing with Nature, reading the words of ones who have mastered their own minds and lives, just sitting quietly and listening to your intuition and your guidance from your own heart, knowing your mind and breath are directly connected and you can control your mind, just by controlling your breath.

Contemplation means to allow something to dwell in your consciousness until it reveals its essence to you. This process alone can answer any question you have. All the answers to all your questions are right within yourself, as God manifests right in your own heart and mind, which gives you direct access to unlimited knowledge and the power of God.

The lie that religion told so that they could keep power and control over people was that we are separate from God, and we must seek God outside ourselves through a go-between, like a priest. Nothing could be further from the truth, as you have direct access to God, because God has become you. We would not exist if God did not breathe life into us, and make His, Her, Its home right in our own heart. Think about this, if you breathe out and don't take a breath in, this life of yours is over and you are a bag of worthless bones. God literally is the breath of life and we literally take life in with each new breath. God rides on the breath. We are one with God. When they say the truth will set you free, it is not the man-made stories, but these eternal principles that have been around since the beginning of time and known and practiced by only the rare few. It is a new day for everyone. The days of the priests, doctors or leaders being the only ones with the knowledge and information and making everyone go to them to be told how to live their life *is over*. Everyone has as much access to knowledge and truth as any other individual through the flow of information, mainly due to the Internet. All these institutions are in decline and in turn, the average person has been empowered. This is what gives us hope for this world.

I spent countless hours reading these priceless books on yoga, the mind, consciousness, meditation and daily readings of my correspondence course. It was the best thing I could ever have done for myself. I feel like the freest, wealthiest and happiest person alive. And I truly know peace and happiness for the first time. Peace of mind is the most incredible gift and to be able to live my life in that state is beyond anything I even knew was possible. That seven-year period in Newburyport was such a healing time. It renewed my soul and my heart. I loved my many walks (especially with Michele) around this special little town and I was always being drawn back to the river and the boardwalk. I had made a decision to put my health first, before anything or anyone. And when I say my health, I mean my mental, emotional, physical, and spiritual health, which are all connected and are all one. It was one of the best decisions I ever made and paid off big time for me. I am so glad I did not listen to the ones who said: "You can't live like that; you have to do this; you should do that; that is the wrong way," blah, blah, blah. For the most part these people are still stuck in the same spot with the same limited and negative thinking where I left them many, many ago. They are still in that small prison. Dare to think big. Dare to take a chance on yourself, which is really not taking a chance at all, as you are in God's hands and God is waiting for you to ask for more and to take you to the highest levels. They say that God is not only able and willing to give you the life of your deepest dreams, but that God is actually 'eager' to fulfill your deepest desires. After your wildest dreams come true, you find yourself completely content living in the present moment and simply 'Being'.

But for me, I first needed to master the physical world and learn how to create anything I wanted, as that was part of my education on the path. Then I didn't have to worry about the mundane things of life, like money, and I could focus all my attention on knowing God. There is no right or wrong, it is all about what you want. I have created the life that fits me perfectly and as it says in the 12-step program: "To Thine Own Self Be True." The writers of the original 12-step book said the purpose of the book was to help you find the God of your Understanding. And so is true with my little book of tales.

I have always wanted more and to keep continuing to grow and expand on this path. I love the statement that says, "What guarantees your sobriety is your continual spiritual expansion," which is how I live my life today and how I take every breath. This is what feels natural to me now. I know in my heart that 'Life is in every Breath'. Most of my life I lived in anger, hate, fear, depression and all the rest of the negative feelings that felt so naturally to me, at that time in my life. If a simple man, like me, can live in a whole new world of health, happiness, peace of mind, abundance and feel that this is the natural state, imagine what you could do?

My practices truly began to bear fruit with inner treasures and also all the outer pleasures and comforts of the physical and material world. The practices of reading the principles of Truth, meditating, solitude, spending time in the silence, contemplation and communing with Nature have truly paid great benefits. The statement, "Your conscious practices will cause subconscious development," literally changed my whole inner being and it was happening before my eyes. I was no longer the person I had been in the past. I did not think in limited negative terms. I now believed in all possibilities. I did not live with violent outbursts any longer. I believed in choices and I did not believe in being a helpless victim that was stuck with undesirable karma. With the right tools, you can actually modify or even change past karma. Your thoughts, feelings and attitude are creating your future karma. I took responsibility for myself and stopped blaming people, places and things for my life. I learned to master my own mind and gained control over my thought processes and learned how to use my heart (called emotional thought) by 'thinking with my heart' to create an incredible life.

Today the best scientists are viewing Consciousness as a massive computing system. It all seems to come back to one story. I was to learn, how as a child, you are like a computer with a blank hard-drive that gets programed. And in my case, I was programed and conditioned with mostly misinformation and misconceptions about life. Many things that I was taught growing up have turned out to be the complete opposite of the truth. A good example of a misconception is that Love is blind. Actually think about it; it is hate that is blind. The concept that you are foolish if you are thinking with your heart, which is called emotional thought, instead of your head, is actually the complete opposite also. When you are thinking with your head you are coming from your limited, conditioned, programed, reactive, conscious mind with information gathered by it's limited five senses. When you think from your heart, you are coming from your sixth sense, which is God, and your intuition is divinely directed. When you come from your heart you are connected to the Cosmic Computer, which knows and is connected to everything.

Scientists have proven that the heart is the most powerful electromagnetic power in the body, much more powerful than the brain. The quantum physicists have proven through scientific research that through your feelings and emotions in your heart, you can actually change your DNA and change the atoms in your body and environment. This is the secret for acquiring the ability to heal yourself and change your life to be whatever you want it to be. The heart has a computing system directly connected to Universal Intelligence and there is nothing that compares with this in the conscious mind.

The language of the heart (feelings) is a language that the universe understands and responds to deeply. We are part of the intelligence behind Nature, and this intelligence is in every cell of our body. It responds deeply to our feelings and emotions, giving us access to unlimited potential and healing powers. The day that Layne told me that I needed to be open to success with this book, that statement triggered something inside me and I thought: *Why couldn't I have it all? Here I am with the most perfectly compatible, sexy woman in my life, living in a little home base, while I continue to do my yogic practices and physical training.* So I released that intention from my heart and a week later I met Barbara and two weeks later we were living together and three weeks later we were engaged and I was living in her mansion overlooking the river. What appeared to happen overnight really had been the result of the past seven years, of many hours spent in the silence and meditation and the building of this creative energy.

Joseph Campbell and Ram D. R. Butler had spent roughly seven years in solitude before returning to writing and playing their part in the world. I am just realizing that I had done the same process in my seven-year period in Newburyport. When you spend years building the energy through yogic practices, and then you have a strong desire/thought and release an intention, it is very powerful and miracles can seem to happen almost instantly. So with meeting Barbara, this seven-year cycle in Newburyport was coming to completion and this book went on the shelf for the next seven years. Now it is finally time to complete. Barbara was a lot of woman and all my attention went to enjoying fully all the gifts of this beautiful, smart woman and that did not leave much time for anything else. Shortly after meeting, Barbara and I were to move to York, Maine, into a beautiful country home with multiple garages that were more like showrooms for our collection of high-end custom-built cycles. This home had a complete training gym for weight training, martial arts, yoga and boxing, along with multiple meditation rooms. There were even outside training and meditation areas.

I worked seven years on the property and groomed the entire acreage to look like a state park, with stonewalls, Buddha statues, pathways, and meditation spots. I had to look at the ending of this time in my life at this property; in the same way the Buddhist monks create their mandalas. They put so much into creating these beautiful works of art and then one day they just blow all of the colored powder away. It is just a reminder for me that there is nothing to try and hold onto in this life and all we have is the Love we share. One day I said to Shayla that I wanted to clear a place down by the road so we could sit and wait for the Riders when they would make their run to visit us at our home called, Thunderhaven. We had started clearing brush and moving rocks when we began shoveling around the edges of a huge rock. As we uncovered it, it just went on and on in size. When we had finished uncovering this rock, it was ten feet by ten feet and perfectly smooth, a perfectly flat table rock that had been hidden just under the surface of the earth. Shayla and I had our perfect stone patio right by the road. Shayla was amazed to find it and I am so glad I followed 'my inner prompt' and experienced it with her.

Barbara and I spent our time riding our bikes up in the White Mountains. We had the most powerful custom-made machines. It was like a dream come true. I flashed back to my brother Skip saying to me in 1970, at the end of the riding season for that year, which was my first year of sobriety: "We have made it through the whole year without being arrested and we are still in one piece." That was a good year. I thought, *how much my life has changed* and I was sincerely grateful.

Well, back to the story. At the time, I was sixty-three years old and I was the biggest, strongest and healthiest I had ever been at 210 pounds and I was living with having it all. It was all from learning to think creatively. Barbara turned out to be an excellent rider and could easily handle the biggest and most powerful customs, called CVOs that Harley Davidson and Thunder Mountain Custom Cycle have built. Barbara not only gave me the experience of living as a multi-millionaire, she also showed me how easy it would be to create my own financial wealth. With the help of Yogic Teachings, I did create worldly wealth and attracted everything I wanted. Barbara is an exceptionally generous and unconditionally loving individual and I will cherish our time together. Today, Barbara's home base is Los Angeles. She loves California and is playing her part for many people out there. Barbara and I were to spend an amazing 'seven years' in Maine together and that could very well be one of the stories in my next book.

Our seven years in York, Maine, has come to an end as of last October 2016. Once again completion of another seven-year cycle in my life and at this time I am now completing work on this book. Shayla reminded me she was 'seven years old' when I was working on the book. In the last few years, My Father, Dave Nock, Tim, my sponsor from the 12-step program, Big Ben, Louise Hay, Wayne Dyer and others that played such a big part in my life have all passed on to the next life. It was kind of another interesting coincidence. Well, this has been my experience after coming to this special little town of Newburyport. You could visit it for yourself and see what secrets about yourself and this place are revealed to you. Or you could just enjoy being here. On a light note, I originally was going to use another name, maybe a pen name, as I was not sure how some of the people from my past might react to these stories. Then I realized that the chance of them reading a book of this nature is not very likely, actually I am not sure how many of them read. I don't think they belong to Oprah's Book of the Month Club. Layne said: "Use your own name, it is a very powerful name. Take Peter (Upon this rock I shall build my church); James (believed to be Christ's brother); and Ford (a pretty powerful name)." So once again, I got the right guidance from God through people.

Thank You God with all my Heart

Barbara and her bike at our country home called,
"Thunderhaven"

TALE OF THE SEVENS

This Tale started out as a joke. That Seven was my lucky number and closely followed by my second number, which was Three. These two numbers were to show up continuously in my life. I was born on the seventh, 12-7-1950, Pearl Harbor Day. I went to Catholic schools for seven years, I drank alcoholically and used the drugs of the sixties for seven years, seven broken noses, my first marriage was for seven years, and my next relationship lasted seven years. Seventh year of my sobriety my high-speed chases with police ended. I spent seven years living a simple life of physical training, reading and doing the spiritual practices. Then the correspondence course I had been studying for seven years stopped being available. At this present time, my relationship with Barbara has come to an end after living in Maine for seven years. The concept that life goes in seven-year cycles certainly seems true in my life.

Well, back to the telling of the tale of the Sevens, which brings up the first memory. There was of a gathering of seven of us drinking and drugging back in the late sixties in a house in East Lynn, Massachusetts. Today I am the only one still above ground. My daughter Rachel said of this Tale: "You should probably call it The Curse of the Sevens." One day I heard what I had saying in jest and I started being open and curious about sevens in my life and the world. They started showing up from multiple sources. One Sunday morning I was sitting and listening to Pastor Shipley, at Unity on the River, talking about the principles of the church called Unity, a church of celebration. And out of the blue she mentioned that the number seven represents completion in the physical world and that number twelve represents completion in the spiritual realm. And then she resumed her talk about Unity principals. I thought, *Where did that come from?* Those were the two numbers of my birthday, the day was seven and the month was twelve. So could that mean that in this lifetime my completion in the physical world (seven) and the spiritual realm (twelve) will come to pass? I've got some work to do then. As soon as I put my attention on seeing sevens, they started showing up all over the place-on the news, in shows, on documentaries, in history, and with people sharing about sevens in their life. I went on line and typed in sevens and was amazed at how many books were available, how many other people had experienced the same inner prompt and had made their own searches in quest of the allusive sevens.

One of the authors of a numerology book wrote, that sevens and sequences of sevens appear more often than any other number. I became fascinated with how these sequences were coming to me from numerous sources and seemingly played such a huge part in the cycle of life. When, I mentioned it to people, they would light up with a smile and eagerly relay a story about sevens, or ask whether I knew about some other seven manifestations that they had observed. I thought *I am going to write a little story about this subject.* Little did I know that it was to be the catalyst for a whole book of Tales that you are now reading.

These are some of the Seven's that I came across, with assistance from Shayla Elizabeth Howell, 'aka Belle'. Our research is as follows:

The following anonymous statement, which I found online, could have been the Foreword for this Tale: "The number seven is the seeker, the thinker, the searcher of Truth (notice the capital T). The seven doesn't take anything at face value – it is always trying to understand the underlying, 'hidden truth'. The seven knows that nothing is exactly as it seems and that reality is often hidden behind illusions." I feel that could have been written for me. I have been blessed to see through the false illusions of this world and see the truth behind the curtain. Basically, what this tale tells us is that everything is just simply connected and right under our noses, in plain sight.

I heard of a conspiracy theory that the great minds like Einstein, Henry Ford, Edison, Nikola Tesla and many others, had made contact with a higher alien intelligence and that intelligence was the source of their advanced knowledge. I laughed. It is true that they did connect with a higher intelligence and that higher source of all creative information is our own Consciousness, which is part of the all-knowing Universal Consciousness. So, in a sense, they did connect with what is a higher intelligence, one that is just alien to most of us. And our connection to this unlimited creative source is our own Subconscious mind. The alien-conspiracy people were right; they just used the wrong word (alien), instead of the word (consciousness). The day I realized that I had gone to the same source, the subconscious mind, as these other successful people had accessed, to bring forth incredible creations, I knew that this book was already a complete success. There is no way you can fail when you go to the very Source of all existence and you can find it, right in the silence. It is waiting for you right now, in every moment.

Well, back to the sevens:

Seven - Your Magnificent seven layer liquid crystal oscillator: Your Heart
Seven continents
Seven major tectonic plates on Earth
Seven seas
Seven miles is the length of Old Orchard Beach in Maine
Seven-mile beach in Cayman Islands
Seven-mile bridge Key West, Florida
Seven bridges in Boca Raton/Delray Beach span sparkling waterways and enhance this luxury resort
Seven miles long is the Mt. Washington Auto Road in New Hampshire
Seven summits, the highest peaks of the seven continents are climbed by an elite climbing club
Seven billion human beings on Earth
Seventy-seven waterfalls flowing into Oregon's Columbia river
Seven-miles-deep – The Mariana Trench is the deepest place in the ocean and much deeper than
    Mt. Everest is high.
Seven hundred years - that was the time it took the gophers out in Western United States to create
    a massive underground network of tunnels. These underground tunnels made such an impact
    on the landscape that it is actually observable from satellites in space. It was a big mystery that
    the scientists did not have an answer for initially. They were to be amazed that this simple
    animal could create such an elaborate set of connected tunnels. The scientists are finding these

amazing locations using satellites. There are over 4,000 satellites that are watching everything on our planet. They can tell if a car door is open with the new advances in optical lenses and super computers. The scientists with these satellites actually verified a fifteen-year-old William Gadoury's discovery. This boy was working on his computer in his bedroom and showed how the Mayan temples in the Yucatan jungle in South America were built and positioned to align with a certain astrology constellation layout. The boy laid the star chart over the map of the temples in this area and the astrology and the temples were a perfect match. There actually was one unaccounted temple matching the remaining star. The scientists got excited and using satellites found the last remaining temple.

Seven Spiritual Laws in the Universe

Seven signs of cancer

Seven Year Itch, the Scientists' research says it is real.

Seven-year cycles, life seems to go in these seven-year cycles.

Seven-years your body will be completely renewed with cells. That is the secret to healing. The intelligence behind Nature is in every cell of your body and these cells (this intelligence) listens to what your conscious mind is thinking and repeating. It you consistently think health and healing, you will have that.

Seven unusual properties of water include, Boiling Point and Freezing Point, Surface Tension, Heat of Vaporization, Vapor Pressure, Viscosity and Cohesion.

Seven strange and unusual symptoms of Multiple Sclerosis

Seven-years - Statute of limitations on most criminal offenses

Seven million was the amount of cash used to buy the support of the local tribal leaders in Afghanistan after the 9/11 attack, by the CIA.

Seven Army Officers that were involved in the special group hunting Bin Laden were killed by a suicide bomber in Afghanistan.

Seven US Federal Agents infiltrated the Mongols Outlaw motorcycle club in operation 'Black Rain' and brought the club down.

Seven signs of terrorism described by our intelligence agencies on YouTube

Seven dead in latest London Bridge attacks

Sevens all through the previous attacks in England.

Sevens all through the terrorist attacks around the world.

Seven countries: General Wesley Clark's YouTube talk about a memo he was given right after 9/11 telling of how our US defense department had planned to invade *seven countries* in five years starting with Iraq. He explained how it was all about oil, otherwise the Middle East would have been treated the way we regard Africa, which is pretty much just ignored. The General's talks on YouTube are full of fascinating facts about 9/11 and the invasion of these countries. The General mentions the mysterious collapse of building Seven at World Trade Center; Seven hours after the two towers came down building Seven came down without ever being hit by anything. The twin towers gets mentioned again towards the end of story, it was just so fascinating to think about.

Seven in Ancient times was the name of the Earth in most cultures.

Seven in Christian Culture is God's number and is considered holy and lucky.

Seven letters from St. Paul to the original churches

Seven Nation Army, an American Rock Duo called "The White Stripes" Seven Signs of the Apocalypse, on the History Channel

Seven Signs of John's Gospel study, which was a simple process for starting Churches

Seven, the God Code, by Hans Lisziam. These are some sevens from his book:

Seventh Heaven
Seven inner heavenly bodies
Seven phases of rain
Seven base metals in ancient times
Seven chakras in the body
Seven chakras in the Earth
Seven endocrine glands and their connection to the chakras
Seven healing colors
Seven substances of the body
Seven cavities in the head

The above are just a snippet of the wealth of information from Hans Liszikam.

Seven colors of the rainbow
Seven notes on a musical scale
Seven is considered the world's favorite number and known as Lucky Seven.
Seven is the most significant number across religions and cultures.
Seven – seven *Abominations of the Heart from Proverbs*.
Sevens from all faiths would fill numerous books; religions seemed obsessed with these sevens.
Seven ages of man, described by Shakespeare
Seven brides for seven brothers
Seven is the number of intelligence in the Hebrew tradition
Seven Great Holy Days in the Jewish Year
Sevens all through Christianity
Seventh day God rested
Seven days in the week
Seven days of Creation (Genesis)
Sevens all through the Catholic Religion (Seven Sacraments)

Sevens all through New Testament, the following are just some:

Seven Spirits of God,
Seven Churches
Seven- "The Holy Spirit" in Scripture was especially spoken of by the number seven
Seven Blessings from the book of psalms

Seven was a unique feature of the Book of Revelation, here are a few:

> Seven churches
> Seven spirits
> Seven golden lampstands
> Seven stars
> Seven lamps
> Seven seals
> Seven horns
> Seven eyes
> Seven angels
> Seven thunders
> Seven trumpets
> Seven kings
> Seven deadly sins
> Seven virtues

Seven was the number of Chronis, "The Greek God of Time"

Sevens all through Hinduism

Sevens all through Buddhism

Sevens all through Islam

Sevens all through Judaism

Seven Sisters (astrology)

Seven Sleepers (Christian myth)

Seven sages (Hindu mythology)

Seventh child to be a werewolf in Galician folklore

Seventh son of a seventh son will have special powers (clairvoyant)

Seventh son of a seventh son in other cultures, will be a vampire

Seven islands of the mythological place called Atlantis

Sevens all through spirituality and yoga

Seven Physic Powers received with the awakening of your spiritual energy

Seven Heavens and Seven Hells explained by a meditation Master

Seventh: In the seventh month of pregnancy, the fetus is believed to be fully enlightened. And then at birth the blinders go back on, the soul goes back into ignorance, so it can experience it's karma.

Seven Years to write the Course in Miracles

Seven hundred and Seventy-Seven quotes from Victor Franco's book; Man's search for meaning.

Seven Dwarfs in Snow White

Seven Magic Mountains, large-scale Desert Artwork in Las Vegas, Nevada

Seven angelic-type UFOs, reported by the Russian Astronauts in 1984.

Seven Light Beings in the tale of the underground city, beneath the rocks carved at the Kailashnath temple, in India. Researching this stone carved temple where people have worshiped for centuries helped explain my love of stones/rocks. Shayla also shares this love with me. Shayla and I will spend hours looking and collecting rocks from the beaches along the rugged Maine coast. There was a Saint from India that would wander the riverbeds at night and be in complete bliss finding these common stones; he treated them, as if they were precious jewels. I feel that I have been in those stone temples many times in past lifetimes. Maybe that was why I was named Peter, meaning the Rock. I was to become friends with Cliff Basford, the owner of *"New England Stonescapes."* Cliff, a massive man, who builds stonewalls with huge, round rocks (some of which are two hundred pound) and he does it all free hand. They magically all come together for him and if anyone is in the flow or the zone, it is Big Cliff. Cliff uses no cement and these massive walls are a work of art. So, the first name that comes up if I am going to mention rocks is Cliff's. Cliff is the Master Stonemason and old soul. With, a rare person, I will have a 'knowing', an inner belief, that I have known someone from past lives. Cliff was one individual that I know we have shared many lifetimes and today we share a great friendship. We both are reaping the benefits of lifetimes of spiritual practices in this life. We both are at a great place on the path. Shayla has decided she is in on this project and it is now 'our book'. Shayla contributed this little gem: Why was six afraid of seven? Because seven 'ATE' nine. Shayla is a pretty amazing little soul. Shayla has been such a gift for us.

Seven all through sports:

Seven Wins, Tour De France, Lance Armstrong

Seven times, Mr. Olympia, Arnold Schwarzenegger

Seven games in World Series

Seventh-inning stretch in Baseball

Seven is the final game in a best-of-seven series, in numerous sports

Seven - There are two seven-mile runways for the space shuttles in New Mexico.

Sevens - All through the Harry Potter series with *twenty-two seven sequences*, including his team number was seven, seven secret passages, Voldemort split his heart into seven pieces (Horcruxes). I guess J. K.Rowling has a thing for sevens too.

Seven Lucky Gods in Japanese Culture

Seven – According to Vedic and Hindu philosophy, every Yogi goes through

Seven stages of development before achieving liberation.

Seven time's believers walk around the Kaaba at Mecca, the holy site of the Muslims.

Seven times the bride and groom in the Hindu wedding party walk around the holy fire and then take *seven steps,* while repeating *seven vows.*

Seven Valleys is a book from Persia describing the *seven mystic stages* of which a seeker must travel to God.

Seven of the crew of the Pocahontas (plaque at Old Hill Burial Grounds) that was where I had my past life experience with Layne.

Seven - Shayla, my granddaughter, at seven years old has formed her first girl band.

Seven times higher energy level than any previous machine, the Hadron Collider is a *seven-mile* circular device going one way and a second *seven-mile* circular device going in the opposite direction and colliding beams of high energy protons for a scientific experiment, at CERN, in Switzerland.

Seven – *seven* miles going in one direction and *seven* miles going in the opposite direction from the center of a military base, to experiment with DNA reactions. Gregg Braden described this in his book, *The Science of Miracles*. Seems like the scientists, novelist and the military have a thing for sevens, too.

Seven astronauts were temporally stranded on the space station at the same time that seven Russian sailors were stranded on mini-sub in the Artic Ocean.

Seventh cycle of fifty-two days is 364 days - one year

Seven Siblings: My father had five brothers and one sister and I am his third son. Once again my numbers appear seven and three.

Seven Wonders of the World fascinating side story about one of the *Seven Wonders* of the World: The Taj Mahal was constructed as a mausoleum for the Shah's wife who had died. It took twenty years to build and put the kingdom deep in debt. When his son took over power, the father was deposed and put under house arrest in a tower of the Red Fort at Agra. All he could see out of his jail window was the majestic resting place he had built for his wife. That would have been the best gift to me of being able to see her resting place and not a punishment.

Seven Wonders of the Ancient World

Seven Natural Wonders of the World

Seven years was the length of time that the wealthy in Europe would keep on their estates a monk-type hermit, as a symbol of their wealth

Seven - every seven years in Israel they would not plant any crops to give the soil time to rejuvenate

Seven Signs: A horror movie

Seven - The Magnificent Seven movie

Seven years and we will have another total eclipse of the Sun across the USA in 2014.

Seven Wonders of Nature

Seven miles up river - Niagara Falls was originally seven miles down river and has moved back to seven miles upriver in the last 12,500 years

Seven Wonders of the Underwater World

Seven Wonders of the Industrial World

Seven Ancient Wonders of the World

A little comparison made between the Seven Ancient Wonders of the World versus the Seven Modern Wonders of the World: One interesting comparison was the Statue of Zeus around 435 BC to the 5.5 ton Solid Gold Buddha in Bangkok.

Seven - Lucky Seven is a Maine-based Model Engineering Club.

Seven-digit numbers, evoking the numbers tattooed on the arms of the Nazi concentration camp prisoners at the New England Holocaust Memorial.

The following has some sevens, but it is a little off topic: I had an unexpected diagnosis the other day, and I was led into room *seven* for the talk. I will have a procedure done this Friday and then in *seven* days I will get the results on *7-7-17*.

What was a hard lesson for me to learn was that two things could seemingly contradict each other, while both being equally true. On one hand, I know that thought is the only creator and that if I am constantly focused on health I will have health. What is also true is that we have our karma (stuff) to experience. If our time in this body is over, God will use some way to bring us home. That vehicle, if your time is up, could be a punk putting a bullet in your head, a car crash, or some type of illness. So, on a lighter note, just in case it is my time to leave this body, I am hustling to finish this book and give everyone a good laugh and more important, to make sure everyone gets recognition for all they have done for me.

I realized very early into this book that it would not be much fun reading if there were too many facts. Originally I had fifty pages of number sevens, having shown up from all aspects of life and the world. And it had turned into more of a technical book than a lighthearted read. It may not seem like it but I dropped most of them. Once you read this Tale you might start noticing for yourself all the sevens starting to show up. It is just how life works. You see that your life has been made up of seven-year cycles. These seven-year cycles are explained in detail, by D. R. Butler (Ram) in his correspondence course called *Living in the Truth of the Present Moment.* It might sound like I am promoting Ram's course and the truth is that I owe much of my personal development, including most of my vocabulary, to the course that he has written over these many years. I owe Kay Butler for the editing of this book and for all the work she did making it into a readable, flowing story. So, really Ram and Kay are the source of any success I might have with this book. If someone benefits by only a tiny fraction of what it has done for me, they would be richly blessed.

So, I hope this tale of the sevens is not too boring, but somewhat thought provoking. Let me leave you with the following Sevens to ponder: Seven World Trade Center (7 WTC) refers to two buildings that had existed at the same location in the World Trade Center site in Lower Manhattan, New York City. The towers were built in 1973. Those are my numbers seven and three that just keep showing up in my life. Seven hundred injured in the first attack on Twin Towers. Seven hundred million dollars was the amount of property damage in first attack on Twin Towers. The planes used in the second attack on 9/11 were 737s', my numbers again. One of the hijacked planes was American flight seventy-seven. The third tower, known as Tower Seven, collapsed Seven hours after the twin towers collapsed. In Tower Seven was the headquarters for all the various intelligence communities' secret information gathering center, which controlled all the information regarding Terrorism. There were a lot of secrets held there. Conspiracy theorists have argued that the third tower was brought down in a controlled demolition. A group of architects, engineers and scientists say the official explanation, that fire caused the collapse, is impossible. Architects and Engineers for 9/11 Truth argue there must have been a controlled demolition. Maybe someone did not want to take the chance of having all his or her secrets exposed. It does make you think about that possibility, just something to ponder. Actually, I think it would have been a smart move; you always want to cover all your tracks, if you are living in the world of secrets.

I am so grateful that today I have no secrets. Your secrets keep you in your own personal prison. In a sense, this book has been a purging of my past life and a release of all inner struggles. I can never repeat enough the power of writing stuff out. You can just write freely knowing no one else is going to see it and that it is all for your benefit. The freedom that comes with this kind of rigorous honesty is priceless for giving rest to the tortured soul. The greatest gift is to walk the Earth as a free human being. I am finishing the writing of this story and another coincidence today September 11, 2017 is the anniversary of 9/11 attacks.

For whatever reason I had a need to write this book and get it out of me. Pain is the touchstone of spiritual growth and the pain keeps returning forcing me to write this book. I had almost completed this book three times and each time I tore it up. I wanted to stay invisible and unknown. I never trusted people and the last thing I wanted is for anyone to know my secrets. And then that ache, that inner prompt in my belly, would return. And then the stories would just start flowing out of me again. So, I surrendered to this process. Gregg Braden had mentioned that when you get an inner prompt to do or create something, that it is something that someone needs and to follow your guidance. Gregg felt it was one of the best ways of service to others that we have available. I choose to believe his conception and it does feel good to think this book is going to serve a purpose for someone. I have since realized what an honor it is that God used me as the vehicle to tell these stories. This is really God's book. This really is everyone's story and everyone's book. To some degree we all go through the same joys and the same struggles and disappointments in Life. All life experiences are to awaken us to the true purpose of life and to eventually return us to our own heart and the source of all Love. What people want is simply to be known, accepted and loved for who they are. This book has been my way of receiving this acknowledgement, acceptance and love of my fellow man. Somebody or something wants these tales told and the sooner it is completed, I can get back to my simple life of riding and meditating in the Mountains.

You might think it is silly, seeing the connections between these God incidents (not coincidences), but if you just start to notice these simple things, that we overlook most of the time, you will see a way to connect with Divine Providence. It is true that God is trying to give us a win in every situation. We just have to be aware of these little, almost insignificant hints. I am in awe on a daily basis seeing God working in my life and taking care of my every need and also giving me everything that my heart truly desires.

I originally thought this Tale of the Sevens was the big story for this book. As it turns out it was just the vehicle to get these other tales written. Martha W., a sweetheart from a NH meditation center, was another tremendous help in getting me started with this book. Martha had said: "All these seven sequences is just showing you how everything is connected." Martha, Katherine, Faith and Eleanor from the meditation center were all so kind to me and they will always have a place in my heart. When the mind and heart are ready to open, God will use the seemingly simplest things to arouse your interest for you to find a way to return to the Source of All Life.

The purpose of this life is to realize that God lives within you, *as you*, and when you know that God lives right within your own heart and mind, and then your search for happiness is over. The God that you have always searched for is alive and well in your own inner awareness and consciousness. That consciousness is God and is the life force that has given you life. Always remember, you literally breathe in life in each breath. God is riding on your breath. God is the original free spirit rider.

I will leave you with this story of a Meditation Master telling his student not to think about monkeys. The student said, why would I think about monkeys? The Master repeated to the student not to think about monkeys. So, the student left and returned the next day and reported that during his meditation all he could think about was monkeys. The Master just laughed and proceeded to explain the mind to him. In the movie, *The Good Witch*, with Catherine Bell, there is a little girl that is being plagued with nightmares about monsters. Catherine (another breathtaking, dark haired beauty) tells her no matter what you do; don't think about cute little bunnies. The following day the little girl returned and said the monsters are gone, but how do I get rid of the bunnies? So, I say to you, whatever you do don't think about sevens. I am hoping this is a little like the kid's game called 'tag' and I can pass the obsession of the sevens off to you. "Whatever you do don't think about sevens."

Best Wishes to All

My son, Benjamin, my daughter Rachel, and the bike I was buying from
one of the brothers from New York City in the early eighties.

SCHOOL OF HARD NOCK'S

This Tale is about Hard Nock's Gym, the longest-running gym in this area, since 1960 and is located in Amesbury, Mass. The people who train at this gym were to play a huge part in my spiritual journey and in the motivation of this book of Tales. I am sincerely grateful to one and all for their acceptance and contribution.

The owner and founder Dave Nock was a US Marine, Amesbury Police Officer, bodybuilder and a man with a powerful presence, who was respected by all. Dave had a powerful connection with the Native Americans and also loved the wolves that he felt a kinship with. Something Dave used to say was "Be Confident but not Cocky" and "The more you sweat in peace (training) the less you bleed in war (life)." I love both of those statements.

Jane Nock, Dave's wife, one of my dearest and most trusted friends, is an exceptional woman and a great person. Jane's powerful heart played a huge part in the creating of the atmosphere of this gym and allowing misfits like myself to feel accepted. Jane and I came from the same world of 'Riders'. Jane has lived a charmed and blessed life and is loved by many, as Dave was and always will be. Jane's energy was the calming presence that held the whole operation together and she was one of the beautiful women from the gym. Jane shares the same love for the motorcycles that I do and we actually had a lot of the same common associates from way back in the day. We both are very fortunate that fate took us on this path and to great lives, as many that we knew died way too young.

Dave's son, Erik Nock, was a power lifter, Harley rider and stand-up kind of guy, who also played a huge part in all the operations at the gym. Erik's connection through Nature was the way he experienced this universal Presence, and he said his church was Plum Island. I could not agree more with him, as I have a deep love for the experience available by the ocean. I have been going to beaches since I was very young. Many times it has saved my sanity.

Erik would sit out on the beach of this island, with his dog by his side and a cooler full of cold ones and experience the presence of God, as much as any of the self-proclaimed religious leaders, probably experiencing much more. Erik and his training partner Mike would be consistently training every night and that is the kind of dedication and consistency that runs as a theme through this gym.

Many members have trained daily at this gym for twenty; thirty, forty even fifty years and they do it without a lot of talk. No big show, it is just 'a way of life' and they just simply do the work. The expression less talk and more action applies to this gym and they are my kind of people. There is an expression in fighting about who is "pound for pound" the best fighter. Another expression: It is not the size of the fighter but it is the size of the fight (heart) within the fighter. For being a small gym in size (compared to a lot of the fancy health clubs) there are more dedicated, hard-core guys and gals packed in there, training day after day with more heart, than you could find anywhere else. If this statement is true that pound for pound tells who is the toughest, then Hard Nock's rules.

They say you can judge a man by the way he treats his mother, while I say you can tell all about someone by the way they treat the animals in their care. One thing in common among the people from this area (the Nock family, my friend Tyler and his sweetheart Dana, Clint, Sandy, Throttle and my granddaughter Shayla) is how they treat their animals and their motorcycles. They treat them like part of the family. Sonny, the most famous rider in the world, said he did not mind getting up early and tending to his horses care and cleaning out the stalls every morning. I felt it told a lot about this man, who is an American legend, and who has created a philosophy of life followed by many around the world. Waking up in that Arizona sunshine, where he lives, just seems to make everything easier; at least it does for me. In ancient days, the warriors trained hard and rode horses. Today we train as a way of life and ride "iron horses," but it is the same sense of brotherhood as it was in ancient times; man is basically the same as he always was. Like-minded people attract like-minded people. Water seeks its own level and I always liked people who did not do a lot of talking, but just quietly took care of business, whatever that business might be.

I was to find the same kind of dedicated people at Hard Nocks with the same kind of love for hard-core training and motorcycles, that I was exposed to at ten years old down in Lynn, Mass. In the early sixties, we had our own Dave Nock's type of a guy, down in Lynn. His name was Tony Pavone, a boxer who trained everyone at the Boys club. Tony shared the same qualities that Dave Nock possessed and helped a lot of us on the right path, despite some of us taking a few wrong turns. Today, my cousin Ricky Ford owns and runs the boxing gym and fight club down in Lynn. A lot of the riders train there at night. Ricky played professional baseball for the Milwaukee Brewers before becoming a local politician. It looks like he will be the next mayor of Sin City. When I was fifteen (1965) my oldest brother Skip, who was friends with all the original members of the new chapter of riders forming around the Lynn area, took me to a Rocky's-type gym in Boston. We all went in the men's room and drank some 'super juice', which I very quietly puked back up. Then we went out and got one hell of a workout. I must have kept down enough of that jet fuel, as I was flying. I had found something that would be one of my lifetime addictions and that was hard physical training. I was instantly addicted to the chemical rush that comes from pushing yourself physically.

When I came to Hard Nocks, I had begun to re-train some of the different fighting stuff I had learned over the years from some very accomplished fighters who had climbed in the ring with some of the top boxers and martial artists at the time. As the years went on, the guys I grew up with started training in the marital arts and I continued training with them. I always enjoyed that I could deny that I had any type of training, because while I had not been affiliated with any schools, I still got to train with the best. The way the ultimate fighters train today, is the way the guys from Lynn have always trained, as far back as the sixties. Do whatever you have to do to win and be the one that walks away.

I have always lived my life in secret and I never let anyone know anything about who I was, until now, with this book. No more secrets, it does not really matter anymore. Who knows how much longer I will be around, as I have outlived so many already? One day it will be my turn to be in the box with a 'store-bought suit'. I love the statement "Have you made your peace? Today is a good day to die." With this book I have made my peace and I have the opportunity to thank so many of those who played a part in my life. How many people get to do that? When we first started going out, Barbara asked Dave Nock who I was. Dave replied: "I am not sure either, but I feel towards him like he is family and I trust him with my life." After reading this book of Tales Barbara said that if someone wants to know who I am, the secret is to just read between the lines.

I did love that there were so many other riders at this gym. "Live to Ride" was so deep in the core of my heart. My brother Phil has it tattooed in big letters, along with a huge, haunting skull, on his chest. Angel Paul, from California, did the skull tattoo. His tattoo, that I love the best is "FU-K THE WORLD" in big letters across his upper back and shoulders, with black panthers circling the tat. Phil is truly one guy who had the balls to be an individual. He is the epitome of a real, hard-core, life-long Harley-Davidson rider and independent trucker. Phil spent a lot of his time running his eighteen-wheeler out of California and Texas into Mexico and back. I never asked him what he was hauling. After all these years, He is still 'in the wind'. I always loved pulling up to the gym and seeing Erik's Harley up on the sidewalk and watching Joe, who just rolled out of Lowell, Mass., pull right up front, as the sidewalks were for motorcycle parking at Hard Nocks. Jeff H. would pull up with his bike with his absolutely beautiful wife on the back; now that was always an uplifting sight. Jeff D. was known to roll his 120 chopper up to the barroom door and do a full throttle blast and blow out the windows. They are just such a regular bunch of guys. The way the front of the gym faces the morning Sun, with the bikes out front is spectacular. Motorcycles and training seemed so natural to me and I truly love the life I have lived.

I know today that there is a chemical release in the body, with different emotions, and you can get addicted to these chemicals just like external drugs. My drug of choice, in a sense, was danger, and I thrived when my life was right on the line. I lived for that feeling and it actually was the only time I felt alive. I have always been so bored with regular life. Life, back at that time, was all about how you could fight and how you could handle a bike. Nothing else mattered. It was a simpler time, which sometimes I miss as my life has made many turns. Some of the many other great people in this gym were Law Enforcement officers and many from the military and I gained a lot of respect for these people doing tough jobs.

The presence of a strong Native American influence affecting this area is really evident in the way the old simple values of honor, integrity, respect and love for animals and Nature are so prevalent. These qualities you will find at Hard Nock's Gym and are shared by all the members. Dave Nock's influence in setting the personality of the gym was the basis for the atmosphere of respect, dedication and consistency that you will find in very few places today. The Native Americans had such a spiritual philosophy regarding life and a great example was that they only killed what they needed to survive. This kind of spirituality was around long before man created religion. Spirituality was your relationship to yourself, to the God of your understanding, to Nature, to the animals and the people around you. It was something that you just lived and there was no need to create a lot of dogma and controlling rules. I had always felt these values and when I came across the people of this gym, it was such validation that there were still people of honor in this world. I will be eternally grateful to all my friends from this special gym.

I was to accomplish more than I could ever have imagined and a lot of the credit goes to all my great friends at this unique gym. Everyone who trains there is a champion in their own right. The truth is that I would ride off the energy of this atmosphere and the people would fuel my workouts. Sometimes I would pound the heavy bag with punches, kicks, elbows and knees for an hour and never be winded. The leather heavy bag was pretty old, so it was not a big deal the day I split it wide open with an open hand strike, but they did not let me forget that one. I keep going back to the power of writing stuff out and how it gives you clarity and perspective beyond just saying it in words; also you will remember much more, about what really happened (for better or worse).

Once again, it has brought me back to a remembrance of my friend Frank, The Stuttering Bandit. Frank, who was built like a young Arnold Schwarzenegger, unfortunately struggled with a bad heroin addition that he brought back from when he was in the Marine Corps. One time when Frank, Big Ben and myself were training, Frank said, "Peter, since you have grown your beard back, you look… like an Irish author." Did he know… something I did not? With Frank looking like Arnold, with a massive ripped build and along with his stuttering threats to the merchants of, "Give me all of your mon… mon… mon… money," it did not take long for him to get caught. Frank's time on this Earth plane has also been cut short. Another friend lost to heroin.

Today we see all types of so called new physical training programs out there, all of these Combinations and cutting edge techniques, the members of Hard Nocks Gym have used these 'so-called' new training practices since the sixties. This gym is rightly called *old school*. Outwardly, the people of this gym look like and are the toughest physical guys and gals you could find, but none of the ego or bragging nonsense. Just the most regular bunch of stand-up people you could find. It is also where John Cena and his brothers began their training. John always mentions his deep love for the Nock family and this gym. John would become known worldwide for his physical achievements, and even greater is the charity work he does. At the time I was doing some volunteer work and was driving a woman named Crystal to her doctor appointments. She had been in a wheelchair most of her life. She adored John Cena and said that living vicariously through his physical abilities uplifted her. I got her a Hard Nock's Sweatshirt and the next time I saw John I asked him if he would sign it for her, which he was happy to do. John asked me about her and I told him how she goes to all his shows and he smiled and did not say anything. Some time passed and the next time I saw Crystal she told me that when she was at John's last wrestling exhibition at Hampton Beach, John saw her and had her moved right to ringside and that has become her place for all his shows. John went out of his way to acknowledge Crystal and took the time to make it the happiest night of her life. This is the kind of person that comes out of this incredible training place called Hard Nock's Gym. Dave loved to tell the story of how John, in the middle of a workout, would put his fist through the wall and the next day would show up to patch up the wall.

Dave Nock and John Cena, from earlier days

Another example of the kind of person who belongs to this gym is Big Brian D., a 280-pound bodybuilder, wrestler, golden gloves, martial artist and Boss Hoss (v-8 motorcycle) owner. They say that Brian never lost a fight in the Golden Gloves, nor ever lost a match in kickboxing. I had a friend who had just gotten out of prison from up in New York, a big tough kid who worked as a bouncer. One night my friend was drinking and getting a little out of hand, down at a Hampton Beach Club where Brian happened to be. The story goes that Brian picked my friend up and put him down 'gently' outside, still in one piece. My friend told me later, very humbly, that he was grateful that Brian had not broken him in half. That is the kind of stories I would hear about the people from this gym, people who have great physical abilities but do not abuse them.

John Cena's brothers Matt (bodybuilder) and Dan (police officer) were two guys with the same values and respect as John. After watching me train, Matt had said, "You must have read The Art of War, (by Sun Tzu, written fifth century BC). I replied that I had not read that book. Matt was to print out highlights from the book and gave them to me. We had some great talks and I realized that this book was much more than the art of war, but really was about 'the art of living'. The same winning principles in war work equally well in living life. Somehow I knew about this stuff, and I thought it always came back to just one story, the same immutable principles flowing all through life.

Of course, no story would be complete without mentioning Matt's girlfriend Coverly, just the most magnificent young woman and as sweet as she is beautiful. She was always so kind to me. Late one Saturday night, I was training and the gym was empty. John Cena came in while I was doing a workout that was a little different. I mentioned to John that I do some different training on the steel-framed cage, usually used for deadlifting and leg squats. And John replied, "Knock yourself out." So I did my usual barehanded workout, punches, open-handed strikes, elbows, on the steel frame, like it was a punching bag. I was learning how to let this energy flow through me, but not *of* me. A few days later, John's brother Dan came in the gym and said, that John had come home and said, "Who is that guy? He is working out on the steel cage barehanded throwing punches and hand strikes, like it is a heavy bag." Dan replied: "Oh that's just Peter. We watch him everyday pound the cage for an hour." So that is my third 'five minutes of fame', a nod from John Cena.

Something happened for me in this time period that would change my life once again. In one of the other stories I wrote how it seemed like something, or someone else, had been writing through me and I realized this is the third time this phenomenon has happened to me. The first was when I took that reading test, which I wrote about in another story, and I could not be bothered with it so I just blasted through it, without giving any 'conscious attention' to it, (no conscious mind involved) and the test was taken by my subconscious mind (which is 95 percent of our mind, with 5 percent being the conscious mind). I got a perfect score on the advanced reading test. Like most good things in my life, I stumbled upon it by accident. The second time it happened was one night when I was training and I started doing moves that I have never had any training in or knew anything about, at least in this life. The moves began flowing out of me from some other source. I believe my subconscious mind knew it from past-life trainings.

I realized that was how the little Kung Fu Master could do those incredible feats, as he was "not doing" them. He had learned to just be the vehicle for this force of nature to flow through him, in the same way that electricity is the true power and flows through the electric wiring to power the appliances. This force of Nature flows through us unimpeded when we learn to just be the vehicle. The trick is learning how to get out of its way and let it flow through us. It is also what the third step of the 12-step program is trying to show us. So the true education is learning how to be the channel or vehicle for this unlimited power source and how to get out of your own way, which is the limited conscious mind. Just as in Judo, as the big guy is coming at you and you side-step him and then add your energy to his momentum and smash his head through the wall, we add or align our strength with this Universal strength and are unbeatable. Of course, we can also use it for better things than breaking heads and eventually we all realize to use it to give someone a loving hand up. It takes some of us a little longer to learn this lesson and we pay an awful price for that lack of love to others. The technique is that for the first time it is about *'not doing it'*, just being willing to be used as a vehicle for this incredible force of Nature. How cool is that? We have this unlimited potential.

I knew that night that the Master was the one who had mastered *"not doing it."* It is about complete surrender to this universal, unlimited life source and the key is aligning our will with God's will, through complete surrender. Then we have power beyond our wildest imagination. This surrender takes true courage, in contrast to the fact that anyone can pull a trigger, including a runny-nose twelve-year old.

We surrender our will by sliding out of the driver's seat and letting God drive. Once again, we go from our limited abilities to the unlimited powers of God. Most people are too afraid to give up control, but it is a paradox as surrendering at this level gives you amazing power. The other principle that I talked about in another tale was of being on your computer, but not on the Internet, 'just our limited self', and them going onto the World Wide Web and having access to all the information, 'just like, when you align with the power of God'.

So I realized that what was happening in my writing of these Tales was not something new, but actually the third time I had been completely out of my own way and a pure channel for the intelligence and unlimited power behind Nature. From writing these stories, I saw exactly how to master this principal, at any time I want. One purpose for this book is to freely share all of these wonderful gifts I have received for those who might be interested. You just feel so happy and complete you need for nothing, because in a moment you can draw to yourself anything you need or want by a simple thought or feeling. Just create the feeling inside yourself of 'already having it' and the universe is 'compelled to give it to you'. The universe is not only able and willing, but it is 'eager' to fulfill all your dreams. The universe wants to give you a win in every situation. We just have to be willing to stop listening to all the old negative programing and be willing to take a chance that there is more than what we have experienced in the past. Be willing not to go by appearances, but to dream about what you want and let nothing stop you. When you adopt this way of thinking and believing, you truly live in a new world of health, happiness and prosperity. Well, the point is you feel so richly blessed, you feel that you are overflowing with all good stuff, that you just want to give and share all of these gifts with everyone, as there is an endless bounty, enough for everyone to bask in health, happiness and abundance. On a lighter note, yes, my humbling has been completed, I have become the person I have always made fun of, that kind and happy person that seemingly lost their mind, lol.

Back to the story and how the combination of this spiritual energy connection from yoga, the perfect gym to train at, the perfect healer coming into my life, my secret places for contemplation and meditation and the perfect places to commune with Nature all came together like a perfect storm. Dave Nock and I became instant friends. Dave remarked that at another time in our lives, if we had met, things could have been completely different. As I said, instant friends and we both knew without a doubt that each other's backs were covered. Dave was known as a hard-ass cop and I never cared what someone's uniform, group colors, size, title, or position in society was. They meant nothing to me. I am glad that we met at that time in our lives. Besides the great friendship, Dave played a huge part for me that I had not had in the past. He was a supportive mentor, a part that I had never received from others, of seeing my potential and encouraging me to keep heading to my fullest potential. That gift from Dave was a priceless gift and I will be eternally grateful for the time we shared. It is a priceless gift when someone believes in you. So as Dave would want, Pass It On, and give someone that special gift. I was to reach my fullest potential through the energy and support of this gym. I was to reach 210 pounds and in the best all-around shape of my life. The pro-boxing trainer told me my punches and strikes were as fast as the middleweights, he trained. Big Chris, after watching me do a series of punches and strikes remarked that no one would still be standing with punches that were that hard and that fast. Dave told Chris that he thought I could take out just about anyone that they knew and Chris said: "You are probably right." I never really saw myself in that way, as it was just all about seeing what I could do to develop these newfound abilities. All the physical training in the gym that I would do was for health and fun. If I had to defend myself, I would just use one of the weapons that I loved. I did love the power of weapons.

Through Grace, I don't live in that world anymore, that hell that all started in my mind. I always saw the potential and incredible abilities of the other people in this gym. There are many from this gym who deserve much more credit than I do, for their abilities and dedication. Naturally, John Cena, being a world-known celebrity gets the lion share of the attention, but there are many equally successful people training their hearts out in this gym. In my eyes, every one of them is a champion. The potential of the people at Hard Nock's gym is unlimited.

Chris W. introduced me to Big Harold, a retired 300-pound enforcer for the boys in East Boston. I knew of Harold and his buddy Kenny's ruthless reputations even down in Lynn, long before coming to Hard Nocks. Harold and I became instant friends. After Harold had seen me in a 'little altercation' at Salisbury Beach he said that Kenny C., Harold's partner in crime, a 280-pound wrestler and leg breaker, would have had a tough time handling me. Harold also said he would back me up anywhere, at any time. There is such a powerful rush, knowing a guy like that would fight to the death backing you up. As Jeff from Newburyport said: "Harold's the real deal." Harold's time on this Earth has also ended. When a man like Harold does the bad walk all his life, he will come to a crossroads; he will take a look at his life. He will either decide to go for one last big score that would set him up for the rest of his life and if he gets caught, then society will feed and house him for the rest of his life. Or, he will hang up his guns and try to live a quiet life. Harold had a granddaughter that he loved seeing, and I was hoping and encouraging him to make this transition. The third option for these guys who walk the bad walk is that they die, which was how it was to be for Harold. His granddaughter had touched his heart, but he just could not make the change in this lifetime; maybe next. They say that we live thousands of lifetimes. This eighty or ninety years I may live in this body is just one day in the life of this soul, called Peter. The soul is eternal and that means forever. Our eternal soul is who we truly are and the essence of us that lives forever.

A friend known as The Greek, from the old days, was trying to catch up with me and he knew I trained at Hard Nocks. The Greek left a couple messages at the gym and finally we reconnected. In the criminal world, there are all types of groups, like the bikers, the Irish boys, the Italians, major drug dealers and the gamblers. The Greek was the only one who could walk into any of these groups and not be challenged. He was treated with the utmost respect in all these worlds. He looked like a massive Queequeg, the tattooed Indian Harpooner, from Moby Dick and had the complete blessing and backing from the top dog who ran New England crime at the time. I never knew why guys like this always accepted and liked me; maybe because I always saw them as good guys who were just misunderstood. I laughed when I thought about the people at Hard Nocks seeing The Greek, looking like he just walked straight off the set of Moby Dick and asking for me. I realized as I wrote this why I liked these types of guys. They were the truest friends you could have and would back you up, no matter what. You just did not want to screw with them, as it could be fatal.

I was training on the cage one night and one of the State cops came by and made a remark about how he would deal with me. He would just get his gun. I smiled and calmly said, "Go get it" and he said, "What?" I said, "Go get your gun, let's find out what will happen to you when you point a gun at me." He tried to make a joke about it and walked off. I have always loved putting my life right on the line. It was the only time I felt alive. My addiction to danger may someday cost me my life, but in the old days it was the only thing that made life worth living. There is a whole science to guns, known to only a few. Guns are really overrated, as are the people who carry them. For the most part you can call someone's bluff and with the others, you just take it away from them. It is an easy technique to learn. You will never see a gun being shown off by a guy who uses guns. It is always the guy that is all talk who is waving it around and trying to be bad. Beware of the quiet one, as the loud mouth tells you all about himself, so no surprises with him. But still waters run deep and the quiet one is probably carrying lots of surprises. You never know who you are dealing with when you come across the quiet one. They say some guys actually get an erection when they pull the trigger. Well, we don't need Doctor Phil to analyze that one. It is pretty obvious, with sex and violence coming from the same part of the brain.

Something else that is very interesting about guns is that having a gun 'will create the need for a gun'. What we have our minds on will draw to us the situations and people, which we are thinking about. Our thoughts will create the very thing we fear. And fear being a strong emotion will increase the magnetic response and bring the situation to us even faster. Think that you are living in a great big wonderful world, full of only great people and you will live in that world with me, no need for a gun. The troubled individuals will not be present in your life. Change your thinking to positive and they just won't be there. All meditation is just concentration, so what you are concentrating on (thinking about) you will create. What you meditate on, you will become. Thought and concentration are that powerful.

Back to the tale, when I was in that space of 'no mind', I could work out on the steel cage with no gloves, throwing punches, elbow strikes, open hand strikes and back fists and not have a mark on me. I had become a clear channel for this energy to flow through me and my hands and arms were untouched, just as the electrical wire is unharmed by the electricity.

One day Dave asked me if I would do my workout on the cage so he could show some kids the power of focus. I knew I was not in that space of 'no mind' but I would do anything for Dave, so I did my usual workout that day. A couple days later, Barbara let out a yelp and said, "What happened to your forearms?" I looked and they were completely covered in black and blues. I hope the guy who walks on the hot coals is in the space of 'no mind' before he does his thing. That would not be pretty. I used to do a series of straight punches on the steel cage, rapid fire, and one day Dave came from the back room and said, "It sounds like there is a jackhammer in the gym. Is that really you doing that, Peter?"

I had been training on the heavy bag and would pound it every day, seven days a week. One day, Dave said, "I see how you train and I am bringing something in just for you." He brought in a huge piece of training equipment that resembled a massive green man. It had been a gift to Dave from Big Mike, from Portsmouth, NH, a giant of a man with extensive martial arts training (powerful combination). It was such a great gift and I would train for hours on it, especially when I would come from a session with White Feather, where I would feel like I could just train on all day, effortlessly. One day, I had the 160-pound green man by the throat and lifted him off the floor with my right hand and had my other hand ready to throw a straight punch and I yelled to Dave, "Pay your F-cking gym dues." That brought a smile to Dave's face. One morning I had been pounding the green man with a series of left hooks when his head came right off the top of his body and rolled over to the door. Oops, he was never the same after that. They never let me forget that one either.

I had a couple of goals when I came to Hard Nocks: doing leg squats with eight plates, 405 pounds (which I did do) and the leg press at 1,000 pounds. Well, as it turned out I easily did 1,350 pounds, for five reps one day. Everyone at this gym makes incredible accomplishments and I am just one of many.

The Author at 63 years old

The Author three years later at 66 years old at Cider Hill Estate

I give all the credit to the Nock's family and the people of this gym, because it was the atmosphere pervading Hard Nocks Gym that is responsible for my reaching my goals.

The best shape of my life at 66 years old

I had learned a technique in yoga where you can put your mind into something and take the qualities from that thing. I put my mind into Dorian Yates's horse legs (a world class bodybuilder) and mentally took all the strength from them and then pictured and felt the strength in my legs. Then I did my set on the leg press. What the mind believes will be true for you, and I believed that I had taken Dorian's strength. I easily did 1,350 pounds on the leg press that day.

There have been so many great friends: Matt, Gino, Larry, Dennis, Lenny, Suzanne, Sean, Dave, Chris, Phil from Newburyport, Jeff, Joe from Lowell, Fish, Tony P, Ben, Dan, George F., Gina, just to name a few. Joe from Lowell is a guy who kept a low profile, who would never let you know that he is one of those all-around best-trained and knowledgeable guys regarding all types of fighting techniques. Joe quietly offered to show me different tips and I will always be sincerely grateful. I was sixty years old at that time and I reached my goals and much more. I was 140 pounds in the sixties, all drugged out and for me to reach 210 pounds in the best fighting shape of my life, as fast as a middleweight, just shows the power of intention, will, repetition and the great support I got from the Nock family and the great friends from this positive, energized, exceptional gym.

I came into some money at that time and I was going to buy a new car. I remembered the little sweetheart Ellen, with whom I had spent three of the best years of my life. She had given me a substantial amount of money back then and said I did not have to pay her back. I remembered her kindness and thought *I am going to send this money to her,* instead of getting the car that I needed. So I sent her the money and right afterwards Dave P., a massive bodybuilder who was a 'Born Again' Christian, came over and said his mother was getting a new car and he wanted to know if I wanted her old car. It was a mint Grand Prix, a really nice car. I thought, *great, I just sent all my money to Ellen.* My next thought was *well I will just get more money* and asked him how much did he want. He said: "No I am giving it to you" and I replied, "You can't give it to me I will pay you." He said,

"No I am giving the car to you or the deal is off. Do you want the car?" And I said, "Yes, I do want it." Dave said, "It is yours." If you are giving freely from the heart, you never have to worry about receiving. That was an incredible gift from Dave, a true friend. I greatly appreciated this great car. As I followed Dave back to my house with the new car, I was to have a very unexpected experience. As we passed through a beautiful section of New Hampshire's countryside, I witnessed Golden Light coming down from the sky. This Golden Light filtered into every atom and into everything. This light touched the houses, trees, cars, roads and into every cell of every living being. This light continued to infuse all of the five elements that make up the physical/material world. God gave me a Golden Light show of his unlimited consciousness.

These have been some of my experiences with this unique group of people at Hard Nock's Gym in Amesbury, Massachusetts. In the past few years, there have been many changes for a lot of us who are connected to Hard Nock's Gym. I had an insight this morning regarding all of these karmic changes. Picture someone running as the ground behind them is falling away right up to them and the only choice left is straight ahead. The past, right up to this moment, is gone. For all intents and purposes it does not exist anymore, so, straight ahead with your even better, new life.

As I had mentioned, my time with Barbara and the Cider Hill Estate has come to an end. Life is always changing and we just need to keep making the best of our time. Another saying on the wall at Hard Nock's Gym was, "The ones that survive, are the ones that adapt." I will soon be returning out west and relocating some of my motorcycles out there and spending most of the year out there. Out West they are running Choppers, with 427 engines and 600-horse power, running straight headers with no mufflers and they are legal. Sounds like the promise land to me. Soon, I will be swinging into Miami, Oklahoma and adding one of these beasts to my collection. Matt S., a great friend from Hard Nock's Gym, was the first of us to drive one of these monster v-8 choppers down in Daytona. Matt loved it and one of these will also be in his collection of great vehicles soon. It is the future of my new motorcycles. I just love horsepower.

When times get hard, people either give up or they double up and go straight ahead through the difficulties. The attitude I developed at Hard Nock's Gym is, "Never a problem only a Solution." Today my attention is on my new, even better future, which is a life of riding even better motorcycles with more horsepower and in sunny, mild weather, from my Arizona home base.

Well, this was my experience at Hard Nock's Gym and the people that train there. I will always be sincerely grateful for having been a part of this exceptional group. I will leave you with this little thought to contemplate. This is from Ram's course and it goes like this: "We truly are a part of Universal Consciousness (which is God) and God has become us. So, if God has become us, we are one with God, then God's powers are Our Powers; We are like a cup of ocean water, we are still ocean water and have all the properties of the ocean water and when the cup is poured back into the ocean, we once again merge with the ocean and become the ocean. When we still our minds, our consciousness merges back with Universal Consciousness and we are one once again."

That means to me that this unconditionally loving God has not only given me life and unconditional love, but has also given me 'all of its powers' and shared all of itself with me. That is unconditional love. That is the secret, we are not separate from God, but we are part of God and we have the powers of God, right within our own minds and hearts. How loving is this being, that it would so unselfishly give all of its love and all of "its powers" to all of us, and we just need to realize it? I feel like I have lived many lifetimes to come to this moment that I am experiencing today; of knowing I have all the powers of God. I am filled with sincere gratitude. The key to using God's power is to only think about what you want, and feel like it is already real, and don't waste a moment on what you don't want. Straight ahead with making your dreams come true and don't let anything stop you. If you stay focused on what you want and fuel it with grateful emotion and think only in these terms, that it is already real. You will have your deepest desire. We literally breathe life into whatever we focus on and think about.

Give your best and the Universe will give it's best back to you. I was someone that was stuck in the trenches for half my life and all I did to change it and to live with having all the abundance of life was to 'change my thinking' and to repeat over and over only what I wanted in my life. It does take a little while to turn around. It is like being in a car and when you want to turn around and go in the other direction, you must first stop, back up, turn and start in a new direction. Your predominant thoughts and feelings will create a new life for you. All I did was think good thoughts about myself, life and other people and I now live in a new world. There is so much right under our noses and it all starts with just being willing to contemplate that there might be more.

It's all about understanding YOUR OWN MIND.

I experienced true brotherhood and real friendship with the Nock family and the members of this gym. Dave Nock has since passed on to the next world, after a full, purposeful life. Jane told me of how the people of this gym rallied to support her and she was so touched by their friendship and love. Jane has since sold the gym to Dave D., a standup guy, who will keep the same tradition and atmosphere that Dave had created. It was an atmosphere of complete support and of people having your back in this life. Dave D. was the perfect choice and the Gym is in good hands with Dave D.

Just as I completed this Tale of The School of Hard Nocks, I got a call telling me that Dave had passed. I knew I needed to complete this book and get it published as a tribute to this great man from all of us who knew and loved him. Dave wanted no rites filled with gloom, just remembrance of a vibrant life filled with love, respect and loyalty. In his honor, pay it forward, do a good deed, always do the best that you can do and "never stop trying." That is classic Dave S. Nock. He will always be in our thoughts, prayers, dreams, and aspirations, along with our gratitude for making all of us reach and achieve more than we believed was possible for us. "He believed in us, when some of us did not believe in ourselves."

Sincere Thanks from all of us
In Memory
David S. Nock
1938-2017

Dave, Peter and the Keystone Chopper

WHITE FEATHER (MY PRIMARY PHYSICIAN)

My Primary Physician

Some very painful remembrances were coming up and Layne directed me to the perfect healer, White Feather. I had seen a breathtaking picture of White Feather dressed in her Native American attire, with the contrast of her beautiful white dress and her long black flowing hair, along with her incredible beautiful facial features. With her massive Rottweiler, Blue, by her side, it was quite the contrast, like beauty and the beast.

The Nock's family Dave, Jane, Erik and Alyssa, all had an incredible connection with these magnificent dogs many that were rescue dogs. Alyssa was to work miracles on me with her healing talents and give me freedom from past misdeeds that I had never been able to get unburdened from, despite all my efforts. White Feather was a supremely gifted healer, who had studied with one of the last Native American Healers from the Western United States. She also was skilled in many of the other healing arts. White Feather, Alyssa Nock, was the wife of my great friend Erik Nock and the daughter-in-law of Dave and Jane Nock, the owners of Hard Nock's Gym. Erik was the envy of all the guys from the gym, as he was the one Alyssa had picked to marry. Men kid themselves, but the women do the choosing. Alyssa was a woman of exceptional physical beauty, with eyes that would melt the coldest heart and a smile that would light up the entire room.

White Feather with her healing work was to release a lifetime of pain stored in my mind, body and emotions. When you reach a point in your life where you are tired of carrying that 'soul sickness', God will intervene and provide an escape route for you. Alyssa was mine. She asked me who my primary physician was. I responded that no one had been able to help me with these issues that she was now ridding me of and I said, "You are my primary physician."

She told me of an open house that she and some other healers were planning and invited me to come. It was going to be a way to introduce people to some of these practices. I was to have quite the unexpected experience. As I stretched out on the massage table, two of the energy workers, (Marty and Gail) began gently touching my neck and shoulders, which was extremely relaxing. As they laid their hands over my heart, I bolted up with an ungodly pain in my heart and let out a roar. Everyone stepped back and the place got quiet. One of the practitioners said that it was all the pain that had been stored up in my heart from this lifetime and that this kind of work helps to release it. It made sense and I made a decision to do the work with him. This work is so personal and intimate that the thought of this beautiful woman (White Feather) having her hands on me did not sound like a good idea, but God had other plans.

My sponsor in the 12-step program had been in Walpole State Prison with Barboza, the hit man for the Patriarca crime family. My sponsor had boxed Barboza in the prison-boxing club. He said that there would be guys who ran the prison during the day and then at night would cry themselves to sleep. I had witnessed in the past, many times, some of the toughest guys having emotional meltdowns over their past actions, but I never thought my day would come. Everything I had done was completely justified in my mind, but *my day was to come, too.* No one gets away with anything in this land of karma. Sooner or later, you will get back with exact mathematical precision what you have given out to others. You will actually gain compassion for the ones doing the most violent acts, while they think they are getting away with it. They have no idea what is in store for them. God was either very smart for creating this law of *what you do to others, you are really doing to yourself* or God has quite the sense of humor and sits back and lets us screw ourselves. There truly is only one inner self that we all share, so whatever we do to another will eventually boomerang back to us. If society does not get you, what you carry in secret, in your belly, will eventually give you all types of disease. However you do it, you've got to get all the poison out of you or it will kill you slowly. One day, we all will have to make peace for our actions. That is not a religious statement; it is a fact of how our own mind and body works.

On following Monday following the open house, when I was getting ready to do my morning swim from the Salisbury jetty out into the Atlantic Ocean. I began to have this ungodly pressure in my chest. I thought for sure I was having a heart attack. I am not one who is big on going to hospitals, so in a crisis, I go to the place that I have always turned to, the gym.

Alyssa was not usually at the gym at that time of day and when I walked in and saw her I knew it was not happening by chance. I was looking like death warmed over and she asked me if I was all right. I replied, "I don't know what your healers did to me the other night, but I am coming apart at the seams." I asked if she had time for an emergency session and she replied, "Come with me" and took me to her special healing room. She told me to disrobe completely and lie under the sheet and she would be back in a few minutes.

As I lay in this room, with Indian artifacts surrounding me, I had the sense that I was not alone in there. I thought *I have done it again. What have I got myself into this time?* I would have run for the door, but the pain in my chest had almost crippled me, so I just waited to see what would happen next. Alyssa returned and *gently* put her hands on me. I pulled myself into the fetal position and sobbed and wailed in pain for over an hour.

Alyssa later shared with Jane Nock that the session with Peter had been the most intense and scariest that she had ever participated in. She wondered what kinds of things I carried, that could cause that kind of deep intense soul pain. Alyssa told me later that she had been about to stop the session when her inner guide told her to continue. She finished the work on me that day and we were both very glad she did, after seeing the results. Afterwards Alyssa was smiling and told me to look in the mirror. I looked twenty years younger, with a golden glow that you would see in a picture of a saint. We both were very relieved that we had gotten through this first session and we shared a heart-felt laugh.

I began sessions with Alyssa/White Feather on a regular basis and the release of pent-up emotions and painful subconscious impressions continued to be expelled. This work was helping me in ways that I had never found anywhere else. During one session, She gently touched the kidney area of my back and I was instantly in agony. She asked, "What's going on?" I told her that I just flashed back to a time over forty years ago when I had been stomped into the ground (known as being rat packed) by a group of bikers from Detroit, Michigan, with a Boston chapter. I regained consciousness the next day, three towns over and faced down in the mud. The only part of my body I could move without pain was one eye. I had always subconsciously carried that pain in my cells and unconsciously had believed that I would have kidney problems along the way. When I left that day the pain and memory was gone and that trauma was never to return.

I was to see on a sports program, how a few of the NFL teams were using these types of healers to help players who were carrying memories of past injuries, which were still affecting their playing ability, even after physically recovering from the outer symptoms. That pain and memory was stored right in the 'cells' and this is the only way to release it. In another session, she was to gently touch my hip and once again the agony returned with the memory of being on my motorcycle and being run over the median after I had kicked in the driver's door of a car on the highway, over an imaginary slight. Once again she released that pain and it has never returned. Along the way the sessions became lighthearted. She would touch a part of my body and I would wrench in pain. We both would laugh and she would ask, "So what did you do this time?" I will never forget her kindness to me. I had told Dave Nock one time that the way to fight me is to come at me with love and kindness. I have no defense against them and automatically drop my guard. We did many sessions over that year and the day came when there were no painful memories left in my cells. I hated to see our time come to an end. She worked miracles in my life. I believe that she did it is in the same way that the Bible talks about the laying on of hands.

Alyssa and Erik went on to have a baby girl named Cheyenne and Alyssa was not to do as much of the healing work she had always done. Once again, I got just what I needed before the window of opportunity was to close. After these sessions I would often go up to the lake at the base of Pow Wow Hill (believed to be an ancient Native American burial grounds). I would just sit with a thought-free mind and savor the moment. I would have powerful insights after my time in these sessions as my mind and energy were so freed up.

One particular day, as I watched a hawk soar over Pow Wow Hill and across the lake, I remembered how Arnold Schwarzenegger had developed the ability to put the power of his mind right into various muscles that he was training and could actually pump blood into a particular muscle with 'just a thought'. I also remembered the Native American chiefs being able to project their mind into the body of a hawk and see out through the hawk's eyes. I thought, *There is only one mind (universal mind) that 'we all share', so why could I not put my mind, into the mind of the hawk soaring just above me.*

I began this process with techniques I had learned and much to my surprise I began seeing through the hawk's eyes, seeing what he was seeing. He was looking out over the vast expanse of the lake, witnessing the entire landscape, while flying just below the white clouds with the blue sky above. Because all life on this planet shares only one mind, which has become every living being's mind, it is actually an easy feat to master.

In the priceless book *Key to Yourself,* by Venice Bloodworth, she explains that our mind and God's mind are one and the same, by using the example of taking a cup of water from the ocean, knowing that the water in the cup is still ocean water. So is true with our relationship to God. We are a part of God, so God's powers are our powers. We have the power to create through thought and feeling. We possess the most powerful creative device in the Universe: our own mind. Come to know your own inner power and you will enter and live in a magical and mystical new world.

This belief in yourself and this knowing in your heart (scientists call the heart the seven-layer liquid crystal oscillator) will give you an empowerment that is a thousand times greater than what your conscious mind could imagine. There is a field of all possibilities and everything 'already exists' there, just waiting for us to bring it into existence. The combination of the thought, which is the electro pulse that will lock onto your desire in this field (like laser-guided weapon) and your feeling, which is the magnetic force that will draw your desire right into physical existence, has the ability to create whatever you desire. You truly can be or do or have anything that your heart 'truly desires'.

God gives us everything we sincerely ask for and we ask with affirmative thought and with the feeling of gratitude for having 'already' received it. The key is feeling and acting as if it were already real. We do this by affirming: "I am sincerely grateful for this priceless gift that you have already given me." The universal Mind will hear you say that it is already created and will then go about bringing it into your personal physical world. We are a part of God and God responds deeply to our emotions. This Intelligence is always listening to your thoughts and feelings. Feelings are a language that the Universe understands and responds whole heartily to. This intelligence is like the most unconditional loving and unselfish father who gives freely of all its powers. So think good stuff and you will get good stuff.

Once you get even a glimpse of the unlimited and unfathomable power of the mind, you will never doubt that anything is possible. This morning I thought, *I would like to add a couple pictures to my book, but do not know how to do that on my computer.* A few hours later, a man named Ron showed up to visit at the house where I'm staying and out of the blue started talking about inserting pictures into his book. He showed me how to add the pictures to my story and another piece for the completion of this book fell in place. Some might say, well, that is not a big deal. Life is actually made up of the little things in our life and if all these little things just come to you through grace, you live a nice easy life. Those little things that happen on a daily basis, taking care of all the details of my life, are miracles to me.

I was probably the greatest skeptic and it is funny how life has a way of changing us. I have become someone who knows with absolute conviction the authenticity of these powers. These teachings have given me health, wealth, happiness, direction and purpose for my life, just by my willingness to try them. We are made in the image and likeness of God. So if we take the time to appreciate any one of his/her wonderful gifts of nature, mountains, beaches, sunlight, health, love or friendship, don't you think that would make God smile with appreciation, since we share the same nature? Most people's minds are on the struggles of life and they don't take the time to appreciate all of these gifts.

Others might not take the time, but I do. I have made it my purpose to fully enjoy all of God's gifts. If you give someone a gift and they really enjoy it, does that not make you happy? So that is my gift back to God. It is appreciating all these endless wonderful blessings that surround us in every moment. Make the time, as one of these days your time in this body will be over and all your worry and rushing will be for nothing. Instead, make your life something worthwhile by doing the things you love and living every moment to the fullest. In the sixties and seventies, I was jealous, of friends who were living the outlaw biker lifestyle and were happy, doing what they wanted to do. One friend had a sign on the wall that said, *I love the life I live and live the life I love.* You can judge their lifestyle, if you want, but they were being true to themselves and loving their way of life.

I have finally found my purpose in this life and it is just being myself, living in gratitude, appreciation and love. Not too shabby a life, coming from the wild, tortured animal I started out to be in this life.

Thank you God, with my whole heart for my returning home to Source and the wisdom teachings. I am sincerely grateful for everything you have given me, from the huge, expensive stuff to the simple sip of hot coffee during my morning meditation. We have been so blessed by an unconditionally loving God who is just waiting for us to return to him/her/it, when actually we never left God. We just had the delusion of being separate. It was the false belief that we were not one with God. It is time to return home. They say that when we die we will be at peace. I say, "Why wait?" We have all the tools and grace needed for peace of mind right here, right now.

Alyssa had told me that my animal guide/spirit was the fox. At that time I had not seen a fox in about twenty-five years, but that was to change very quickly. The following week I was to see a fox crossing the road ahead of me and a few weeks later I was to see two in one week and it continued with regular sightings of foxes, at all kinds of unlikely places. At the Cider Hill house where I lived with Barbara, we had numerous foxes, old and young, even a gray one. At this writing, I am living in York Harbor surrounded by mansions. I have been having regular visits from the foxes again, down here at the harbor, which seems like another unlikely place. Early the other morning as I was leaving for the beach another fox strutted right in front of me across the driveway with the sun rising in the background. I just smiled to myself and thanked God for my life.

I know that what we put our attention on draws that very thing to us, so some of the sightings may be coming from that. Also, scientists have found that when they look through their microscopes at the tiniest subatomic particles, their *attention* causes these particles to actually 'come into existence'. So some of the fox sightings are from me drawing the foxes to me by my attention and I choose to believe some are because Alyssa made me aware of my animal spirit guide, the fox. The fox is a real survivor. When I see the fox it always brings back the memory of that wonderful healer 'White Feather' and how many of her gifts she has shared with me. It is because of her work that healed me in regards to women that I became capable of having loving, healthy relationships, like the one I was to experience with Barbara.

Barbara and myself on our early spring run to the White Mts.
Eternal gratitude to Alyssa,
an exceptional gifted healer

TIDE MASTER (UNLOCKING THE SECRETS OF THE TIDES)

Unlocking the Secrets to the Tides

This Tale is about my time along the Merrimac River and the secrets that the river taught me. As I have said in a previous Tale, my great friend Jeff Smith gave me a book called *Siddhartha,* by Herman Hesse. I had heard of this book back in my school days and, of course, at that time it was just another book that I never read. It was the perfect time for this book to arrive, as I was having the same types of experiences, being in the presence of this river, as told in this simple but inspiring book. Siddhartha meets the ferryman, Vasudev. I was reading this book at the time that I was to meet a meditation Master.

Thoughts of the river always bring to mind the story of the Indian chief and the young brave, sitting and talking beside the river, beside a blazing fire. The full moon was lighting up the river as the young brave listened intently to the chief tell the following story: Within every person there are two wolves, one good and the other bad and they are always fighting. The young brave asked, "Which wolf wins?" The Chief replied, "The one that you feed." I love this story, as it reminds me that whatever I am thinking about, I am feeding those possibilities. As Louise Hay says, "Every thought we think and every word we speak is creating our future. Would I like this thought to create my life? Would I like to have the experience that this thought could bring to me?" The wolves' story always reminds me of my great friend Dave Nock, who had a deep connection with the wolves and Native Americans.

The writing of this book has really shown me; over and over, how blessed I have been with great friends. Life truly is all about the people in our life and all about the love and friendship we share. Many of these people have always lived their lives in this way. It is such a big deal for me, as I lived with a closed heart. I have mentioned in a past Tale of being jealous of gang members who obviously had love for their brothers, as I had never felt anything for anyone. People would say to me, "After all we have been through, Peter, you look at me like I am a stranger." I would think to myself, "Because you are." I never shared myself with people, so they didn't know me and I didn't know them. Soldiers, after a while in war, can shut down emotionally, as a way of survival. For some reason, I shut down completely and my heart closed at a very young age and remained like that for most of my life. What a sad and lonely existence that was. So to live today with my heart wide open and to share love with people is the greatest gift.

The reopening of my heart began when my son was born and then with the birth of my daughter the following year. These two children were the beginning of my heart being touched in a way I had never experienced. Down the road Ellen M. came into my life and this sweetheart of a woman caused my heart to open even more. My memories of Ellen and our times together will last me a lifetime. I really had to learn that it was safe to love. It starts with having a safe environment and healthy loving people. Years later, the healing techniques of White Feather forced opened my closed heart chakra even more and I experienced all the love that had been locked up in my heart. Shortly after, I was to meet Barbara. She was honest with me and said that the man I had been in the past was someone that she "would never be with," but that she loved the man hidden behind the mask of that emotionless psycho. When you know yourself you know others and that is why I have compassion for those who are living as I did. It is only a matter of time and they will have to come to terms with their life. Then the time for true courage will be necessary. Now you know why I have so much gratitude to the astonishing healer known as White Feather. She gave me the gift and freedom to love. The story of 'unconditional love' continues with the gift of Shayla Elizabeth Howell. Can you imagine how I feel to have a healthy, smart, loving, beautiful, 'normal' granddaughter, after the life I have lived? I had wanted this for Big Harold, the aging enforcer for the mob, who had trained at Hard Nock's Gym, as he loved his grandchildren and they had touched his heart. He did try, but it just was not his time to experience this unconditional love. I am sure next lifetime he will, as he was so close. I saw how his grandchildren had reached in and touched the heart of this pirate and I know his time will come. I truly believe in the eternal Essence of us and that we all eventually will return to love. This is why the conclusion of my little book of lighthearted Tales is, after all is said and done, "It is always about love." I watch my granddaughter Shayla freely giving love to anyone who comes into her world and she would not even know any other way to live. That is from the gift of having a loving, wise mother Rachel, who raised her so perfectly.

What this book is also about is reminding all of us to become more aware of the power of thought. Every culture since the beginning of time has tried to tell us in story and parables the power of our own thoughts. A great example is Aladdin and his lamp. How many times have we heard this story and never knew the true meaning behind it? Aladdin's lamp represents 'consciousness' and the rubbing of the lamp means 'understanding'. The genie represents the 'subconscious mind', that mighty power within yourself waiting for recognition and unfoldment.

Your connection to this divine power is through your own thoughts. You are feeding or fueling and creating that very reality that you are continually thinking about. So, once again, how important is it to be aware of what you are thinking? We are creating our world and our life, in every moment, with each new thought. "Every detail in every moment is the result of our thoughts, feelings and attitude." For me, that is one of the most powerful statements. Just take a moment and think about what those first five words are saying; that we are creating 'Every Detail in Every Moment', which then becomes our life. That makes me really conscious to watch my mind and to control my thoughts. Our thoughts are the only creator. God is simply a law of cause and effect, and our thoughts are the cause. Could it be this simple? What if this statement was true, what would that mean to you and your life? For me, it was the beginning of living in a whole new world of health, happiness and prosperity, a world full of magic. There is no outside force causing things to happen to us by chance or fate. Every bit of every experience is something that we have created though our thoughts, feelings and attitude. Gratitude is the most powerful attitude. With just this feeling of gratitude, you can magically change your life.

Learning how to create your future karma is something of inestimable value. I try not to create very much karma for the future, but what I do create is all good stuff by being kind and loving.

I never want to return to the fetal position, sobbing uncontrollably again over destructive karma. Everything is created from within us and the physical world only mirrors back our own creations. "The outer world is only mirroring back, what we have created within." How mind blowing is that? Take a moment, if you will, and contemplate these last few statements and realize how empowering they would be, if they were true. I live them every day as the absolute truth and can testify to their authenticity, with every fiber of my being. They are so empowering and being someone who hungered for power; I was to find the ultimate power. I did not expect to find that the ultimate power is Love. Ohhhh yeah, have I not heard that all my life, that there is no power greater than love. Well, I am Irish, so it takes a little longer to grasp stuff, plus being hit over the head one too many times, it does tend to slow down the brain function. I am glad I had enough left to grasp this knowledge.

Another way to say this is that 'Every Thought is a Prayer'. When you are thinking about something, God takes that thought as a prayer of something that you want in your life. God gives us everything we want and as far as God's concerned, 'What we think is what we want'. As Ram has said in his course, "If you take nothing else from the course, please become aware and conscious that your thoughts and feelings are creating your life." God is simply a law of cause and effect and our thoughts are the causes. I remind myself that our thoughts are the catalyst that creates a heaven or hell right here, right now, for us. Just with changing your thoughts and breathing deep slow breaths you can change from being in a hell and return to a heaven of 'your own making'. When you have the power to create an exceptional life just by thinking good thoughts, why would you wait and what is holding you back? What holds us back is all our programing and conditioning that we received growing up, when we were forming our beliefs about life. These beliefs can be changed with the proper information and you will know a new world for the first time.

I may have mentioned this story earlier, but in the Peter Pan movie, Peter tells 'the secret of how to fly' and it is 'just think good thoughts'. So simple and actually so true, as all I did to have this great life that I live today was change my fearful, negative thoughts to good thoughts and I live today with all the comforts and pleasures of the physical/material world. So, as Peter Pan says, the secret to flying is to 'just think good thoughts'. Peter James Ford says, the secret to having it all is 'just think good thoughts'. Maybe I will put this on my tombstone. It is either very insightful or completely crazy. When I first read about the behavior of the perfected Masters, I thought the difference between an enlightened being and a psychopath is a very thin line; neither have any limits and experiences complete freedom from man made rules. For some reason, that analogy still brings a smile to my face.

There was a time when I would have laughed, along with most people and made fun of someone talking such silly notions as these. But all you have to do is just try it and find out for yourself. Michele, another breathtaking, absolutely beautiful, black-haired goddess of a woman, had said to me: "Peter you live in La La land" and I agreed. When I believed life was hell, I lived in hell and now I believe I live in a great big wonderful world full of great people, numerous beautiful woman (too many to count) and an abundance of opportunities. Michele was right, I do live in La La land and it is 'as real or unreal' as the life that I had lived when I was struggling in hell. In the past, my response to the statements I have just made would have been: "What I think is not going to affect anything." I believed life just happened without having any control or choices. Basically, that is living the life of the helpless, choice less victim.

Louise Hay has a powerful quote: "What you think and what you believe will be true for you. Your thoughts and beliefs create your life, it is that simple." When I mentioned to my initial contact at Balboa Press, of my love of Louise's books, he said: "How will you feel when your book touches someone else's heart in a similar way?" Wow, that would be the most amazing gift to me. While I am using fantastic quotes, here is one I cherish from Shakti Gawain's book *Creative Visualization*: and it goes like this: "Every moment of your life is infinitely creative and the universe is endlessly bountiful. All you need do is put forth a clear enough request and everything your heart truly desires 'Must Come to You'."

Whenever you continually repeat something with your conscious mind, it is eventually accepted by your subconscious mind as reality. Then your subconscious mind (part of universal mind) proceeds to bring it into existence. For example, if you continually repeat Shakti's quote, it will become true for you, as it did for me and you will watch things come to you seemingly magically. What you think is what you get.

It truly seems like someone else's message has begun to flow through my writings. What was once my stories, have changed to someone else's message and also coming from another source. But they are much more interesting, so I will continue to write and seemingly just be the vehicle for an unseen force. Well, I hope you are enjoying a few thoughts of the 'mystery writer' who has seemed to take control of my stories.

Back to the story and that image of the chief and brave sitting along the river, gives you a picture of the many nights I spent reading, meditating, and just simply being beside my precious river. It reminds me of the love my father had for his walks along the beach. He truly was a good man. It was a much simpler time in my life and as I have progressed in my personal development the part I play in the world has also progressed to a full wonderful life. But like Siddhartha, I crave the simplicity. Soon I hope to return back to that simpler way of life. I have a feeling that after this book is published my life will never be the same again. Whenever I would speak with my sponsor about wishing to go back to a simpler time in my life, he would always reply: "That was then and this is now."

Looking back at the time I spent in Newburyport, it was such a carefree time in my life, I truly had returned to the innocence of a child. I was carefree and had nothing to lose and worried about nothing. I just did a little work, trained four or five hours a day, read inspirational stuff, meditated, and spent time in communing with Nature, swimming in the Atlantic Ocean, with many trips to the ashram.

The Ferryman told Siddhartha, "You will learn to listen and the river would teach you how to do this." This is a priceless gift, to learn how to listen. God is speaking to us all the time and most of us are too busy to be aware of the divine direction God is offering us in every moment.

'God is trying to give us a win in every situation'

'Life in every moment, Life in every breath, God rides on the breath'.

God riding on the breath gives new meaning to the expression 'Live to Ride', which is tattooed across my brother Phil's chest. The gift of the present moment is one of the most wonderful experiences you will ever know and when it happens you realize a whole new world. It takes practice to get to the place that you are actually fully present in the moment, but it is so worth it. Some of the most valuable gifts are some of the most overlooked and underrated ones, but they can make the difference between health or illness, happiness or sorrow, wealth or poverty, success or failure and some of these gifts are:

Knowing how to listen
Knowing how to breathe correctly
Knowing how to think
Knowing how to master your mind
Knowing how to play your role in this incarnation
Knowing how to be still
Knowing how to contemplate
Knowing how to commune with nature, which is inherent in all of us
Knowing how to love
Knowing how to let go of everything, even your very life
Knowing how to live fearlessly in this world
Knowing how to accomplish anything you truly desire
Knowing how to forgive everyone, starting with yourself
I forgive and *'set myself free'*.
Knowing how to simply be
Knowing how to be yourself
Knowing how to be patient

Knowing how to be kind
Knowing how to journal
Knowing how to take personal inventory of yourself and your life.
Knowing how to set yourself free
Knowing how to write unimpeded
Knowing how to be successful at life
Knowing how to be successful at living
Knowing how to create your life just the way you deeply desire it
Knowing how to control your mind, emotions and body
Knowing how to express gratitude
Knowing how to experience compassion

These are just a few of the gifts from self-knowledge that are available for the sincere seeker. They are some of the treasures that have become my life. So much of the simple wisdom of the ages seems to be missing in this present generation of souls.

At this time I had moved in with this beautiful woman, Barbara, in her five-story home that over-looked the river that I was writing these stories about. I was in the best health/shape of my life, with garages full of high end show and go choppers. I thought this is like a dream. I realized it was a dream and it was 'a dream in consciousness'. Just as we dream at night, we also dream (think, imagine, feel) in the waking state. We call it thinking but it is really dreaming. The difference is that what we dream in the waking state becomes our lives. We literally dream into physical existence whatever our hearts desire. I had dreamed into existence the hand of a beautiful woman, a great base camp, perfect health, financial wealth and the motorcycles of my dreams. All I did to have it all was think good thoughts and think about how great life is and to be grateful for everything, even the simplest experiences. I was equally grateful for the sip of hot coffee in the morning, as I was for all the big stuff. God loves a grateful heart and will bestow even more blessings on the appreciative soul. Also, something priceless that my great friend, Kay Butler had said to me was that just because we create something does not mean it is forever. I am so grateful for that piece of wisdom and it made the changes in my life more easily acceptable. When I awoke one day my dream life with Barbara was over and we parted friends. It was just like the dream you have in the sleeping state and when you awake it was like it never happened. We do the same thing in the waking state and I awoke and Barbara was gone. And it was like nothing ever happened. It all depends on your karma and if something's time is up and it has served its purpose it will vanish. So, what I am going to do is dream an even greater dream to experience in this life. It is so easy 'just see and feel' what you want as if 'it is already a reality'.

Back to the story of Tide Master, one of the amazing phenomena that happened to or for me was my first experience of being able to tell which way the tides were going, just by my intuition. As I sat in meditation down by the public boat launch, I realized my very inner being was being pulled into the river, in a clearly distinctive direction. It was a sense of being pulled out to sea. The more I became aware of it, the stronger it got and I thought to myself, *Now what, I can feel the direction of the Tides? I don't think I will be in a rush to share this one with anyone, as everyone already thinks I am crazy.* In actuality, that is exactly what it turned out to be. Not that I was crazy, well maybe that too, but I had become aware enough to feel the activities of the planet, that are just beyond our five senses. Initially, after it would happen, I would go check online the times of the tides and, sure enough, the direction I felt I was being pulled in was correct.

As I learned to sit and experience the feeling of this inner pull, this force continually increased to the point I would feel like I could be pulled right into the river. I did realize later that it really was not a big accomplishment, as the moon's gravitational pull affects the tides, making the high tide even higher and the low tide even lower, especially with the full moon. We are 70 percent water and our brains 85 percent water, so how could we not be affected? It showed me how most people's minds, including mine, are or were so cluttered with endless, worldly information, that they are not aware of what is right here, right now, right under our noses. None of the experiences I have had are really anything special, as all of them are right here for anyone to experience simply by stilling our minds and sitting quietly for a little while. These gifts are part of our own inherent nature. Just learn to become still and the world will unfold itself and reveal all its secrets. Feeling the tides was really just an entry-level experience. It was just a meager beginning, compared to what lay ahead. It was the doorway that I was entering into the vast, expansive, inner world containing many different and numerous types of the earth's activities. If the animals on the islands in the path of the tidal wave, can tell when the tsunami is coming and head for higher ground, how much more with our conscious abilities can we connect with Nature and the planet?

We are a privileged species, as with this divine nervous system we possess we can be 'aware of awareness' and 'conscious of consciousness'. All of life's secrets are waiting to reveal themselves in the Silence. The Silence is the language of God. I know, sounds like another paradox. Welcome to the spiritual path, 'where two things can contradict themselves and both are true'. The stories of Native medicine men and meditation Masters knowing the secrets of life, the earth and the inner worlds are all true. I remember a story of how the Indian Chief would know it was time to leave his body and would go out and sit up on the mountain and enjoy the last moments. That was a gift and sometimes a curse, that I also received and I would know when someone's time in this body was up. I also had a month of mixed signals about myself and whether my time was up, but it has passed and looks like you are stuck with me for a while.

Once you experience, even for a moment, this glimpse into the true workings of the Universe, you will be changed forever. I had said to a swami friend that I was having experiences 'like from biblical stories or tales of seekers from ancient India'. I said: "What is going on? I am nobody. I am not some saint or holy man, how can this be happening?" He gently smiled and said: "Are you sure you are not? We all are experiencing these things, isn't it great?" You are not just some nobody. You could contemplate, in your meditations, about who you have been in past lives. You might be surprised, just what an old soul you are. No one experiences what you are experiencing unless they have done lifetimes of spiritual practices and you will be happy with who you find yourself to be."

I relaxed and started really enjoying this 'knowing' about which way the tides were flowing and learning the secrets of the river. I also noticed a variation with the currents, temporary stillness that turned out to be what they call the ebb tide. The ebb tide explained what I was witnessing about the tides and currents of the water being drawn away from the shore in a slightly different way. There was so much there to see, that I had never been aware of before. I would watch how the tide slowly coming in and slowly going out would correspond to the process of my breath coming in and going out and, once again, see how everything is connected, just one story. I would watch as all the seagulls would face into the wind and how you could also tell which way the tides were going by the way the anchored boats would be facing. I started seeing how the wind would skip across the water and just flip the thin top layer of water over and show you the direction of the winds. That one you had to watch for, as it was very subtle. When I shared about seeing this, with my friend Chris, he said that was one of the ways the old sailors use to navigate.

I was just having so much fun seeing and feeling what most people would never see and also feeling so connected with the unity of Earth, Nature and God. I also thought that the shift with the ebb tide that I had been witnessing would help me with my swimming the mouth of the river, as it could give me a window before the currents shifted. As I wrote this I was reminded how the planet is seventy percent water, our are bodies are seventy percent water, and our brains are eighty-five percent water, so naturally we are all affected, as the oceans are, with the gravitational pull of the moon. I shared my experience with someone and they responded with, "How can you know which way the tide is going?" And I responded, "How can you not know?"

It is such a paradox as these experiences, on one hand, are the greatest things that you could ever experience; and then, on the other hand, it is simply 'just what it is'. It is just nature and all of it just comes naturally.

Once again, everything was showing me how all things are connected. And this is a living planet and nothing is separate. There is only one, which most call God, and this whole world and everything in it and everyone that is on planet Earth are all just part of God's play.

Think about this: One-day your body will return to the earth (you are just dust in the wind) and eventually all possessions go too. 'Everything and everyone' returns to God. So, how could this life be our life and not just the play of God? Something to take a few minutes and contemplate is this mind-blowing statement: The plants give out oxygen, which we take in to live; and then we breathe out carbon dioxide, that the plants take in to live; and once again the plants give us back oxygen. This dance of breath and this cycle of life are like a love affair flowing to us and from us to the plants, giving each other life. This is just, one example, of how we are all connected.

Another cycle of life is how the water drops form in the clouds, and then rain falls onto the mountaintops and then flows into the streams and the rivers and eventually flows back into the ocean and then through evaporation returns to the clouds, to once again become rain and start the whole process over. It is just one amazing big circle of life. No, I did not steal that from *The Lion King;* well maybe unconsciously. This is really God's world, God's life and it is all just God's play of consciousness.

In one of Ram's lessons, he said that *the same consciousness that is reading this lesson* (in 2017) is *the same consciousness that wrote this lesson* in (1975). That statement still puts me in awe of the wonder of God. There is only one Consciousness that has ever existed and has become everything and everyone and is the same Consciousness in the past, present and future. In Consciousness, there exists the past, the present and the future and that is why through meditation you can enter any time period. In a sense, you can use it like a time machine.

We are just the temporary caretakers of God's stuff, including our homes, toys, our bodies and even our children. Of course, I want to be the best caretaker I can be, but always knowing that all of this is very temporary and to live every moment of my life by living the life I want to be living, which today is just God's life. I have created a great life for myself but today I love to say: "What do you have in mind for me today?" This truly is God's play and it is called The Play of Consciousness. Now, we can align ourselves with God, joining our self-will with God's will and make our time here a Heaven on Earth. We can also master the physical and material world very easily, by learning about our true nature and practicing some simple principals. Once, you start to live in this way, you wonder why you took so long to make your life into such a pleasant life.

Now, we also have our karma to burn off, so many changes will continue to happen, but after a while you will have had so many changes that you have gone through that you will know that what comes after the change is moving to an even higher level of personal development. There are so many secrets that get revealed to you as you learn to become still and aware of what is right under your nose. It would take many books just to cover my experiences, which do not even compare with the experiences of many others. I truly am just a seeker and always want to remain the humble student. I want to read and contemplate the writings of these insightful healers and Masters. What happens is when you learn just one principle or just one eternal truth it will answer a hundred questions that you might have had for most of your life.

I hope these stories spark an interest in some ways, for you to start your own personal search or to give you a little fellowship on your journey. I had almost completed this book three times and tore it up thinking that there are enough books out there saying all the same stuff, maybe without my 'unusual experiences', but you never know what simple phrase or just the right combination of words is going to ignite someone's interest.

I know, that this book is full of spiritual energy that is coming not from me, but from the lineages of numerous Masters who have become my teachers and mentors and in some way 'they' are reaching out with this information. So, I am going to finish the book and leave it in God's hands to decide what is to be done with it. I always give all the credit to God and to the people he or she has worked through. That way, my big ego can't grab ahold and make me into something I am not. Krishna Das says that he chants to save his ass and I do my practices to save my ass. Left to my own devices I would probably spend my life in prison. In the twelve-step program it says we do not do this to become saintly but we do it to save our Asses. Not many saints out there but lots of people sincerely trying to do their best. I have played many parts in this lifetime and today I am none of them, just a silly Irishman who thinks he is 'The Yogi of Long Sands'. I walk this magnificent beach in York, Maine, year round and I am so grateful for another beach to walk. Beaches have saved my sanity many times. Actually, some may question that it worked.

Once you become something in this world, get ready to be attacked. It is much more fun and safer being nobody. Let the other people live in the spotlight, as one week the world makes them adored celebrities and the next week the world is tearing them back down, looking for any kind of dirt on them. It is just the way of the world. I always remind myself of two things: Never forget how wonderful it is being 'uninvolved' and 'just passing through'. 'Just passing through' is my great friend Tyler's philosophy. I truly loved my time down at the river, especially the nights. I feel I got to live the story of Siddhartha. Siddhartha's story is my story.

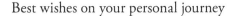

Best wishes on your personal journey

Peter's 120 Race, Harley Road Glide

SHAKTI BURN (TRIPS TO THE ASHRAM)

Trips to the Ashram

This Tale will include trips to the Catskill resort area of upper state New York where the Ashram that I visited is located, in the United States. Also, this Tale will include my trips to the Yogic Centers in Boston, Andover and Cape Ann, Massachusetts and Wilton, NH, along with trips to the Miami and Sarasota, Florida centers. Thanks to all the great people, I have had the privilege to meet and become friends with over the years.

And, I will share how it all began with the reading of one very special book, written by a Meditation Master from India. My oldest brother, Skip, had sent me this book on his return from the Ashram, in India. The book was about the awakening of your dormant inner spiritual power through the grace of a perfected Master. And when I first looked at a picture of the author, I thought, what did my brother get himself into now. To me, the Author looked like the toughest street person from India that you could find, but by the time I finished the book, I looked at his picture and thought, that is the most handsome man I have ever seen.

Just like anyone else, that has been touched by this Master or visited his Ashram, I too, would love to mention his name and the names of his books and special places. But, it is best not to mention specific names because of the way the physical world is today and to preserve the ancient teachings. Myself, just as many others are disappointed in not being able to publicly show their appreciation and gratitude for the part that he played in our transformation. So, I will show my gratitude through this simple book of tales and that is my gift to him. I know that it is this Master's spiritual energy that has given this book life. And, he really gets all the credit for any goodness that flows through this inexperienced messenger.

His spiritual energy, known as Shakti, infused this book and the simple act of reading his words lit me up spirituality to a level like never before. There are numerous experiences, from this spiritual energy called 'Shakti' and one of them is that your face and head can get as red, as a tomato. You can look like you have bad sunburn. So, I decided to use the name 'Shakti Burn' for this tale. I was to have this experience of Shakti burn a number of times and it came from this unseen force. The Shakti (spiritual energy) builds in your body (through spiritual practices) and you can have all kinds of mental, physical and emotions experiences. They call the experience of having a Meditation Master awaken your dormant spiritual energy 'Shaktipat'. That energy, 'a sleeping giant', is located at the base of your spine. This energy will run up your chakras, energy centers in your body and right up your spine to the top of your head, to the crown chakra. Shakti is the name for this spiritual energy and it can give you many different mental, physical and emotional reactions called Kriyas.

As, Arnold Schwarzenegger could put his mind into his biceps or any other muscles and then cause blood to flow into these muscles just by using his mind, you, too, can do the following awesome manifesting processes. The process is putting your mind into your base chakra and then visualize your breath flowing up the spine, while you are saying the Ah sound and let it run right up and out the third eye. Shayla reminded me that I should tell the readers that it is also known as the 'Mind's Eye'. Add your desire to this breathing and Ah sound process and let it ride on the breath and the vibration of Ah. With practice, you can manifest a desire, sometimes instantly and watch it manifest physically. This is another priceless process provided by Wayne Dyer. Wayne gave us this gift of knowledge of the power of the sound Ah, the sound of creation.

As I had said in a previous tale, I believe that on a lower level of intensity I did have my spiritual awakening coming into the 12-step program. But with the reading of this Master's book that was so imbued with this energy, it was like being rocketed into another dimension. I was lit up like a Christmas tree when I went over to my woman friend at the time, Karen; she was a little shocked with my new face.

Karen answered the door and said: "Have you been drinking? Your head looks like a big boy, red tomato!" I looked in the mirror and my face and head were bright red and on fire. I laughed. At that moment, I felt like I did not have a care in the world and knew a whole new world was going to open up for me, which it did and it was beyond my wildest imagination. That is the feeling of what a few drinks does for an alcoholic as he feels a new freedom and a carefreeness that he never knew. It is interesting, how Carl Yung commented, how we use the word 'spirits' to describe alcohol. I learned a valuable lesson almost immediately and it was in regard to the power of the 'vibration' we are putting out and also about 'body language' and 'human nature'.

I, like most people before having an reawakening and opening of my heart, had what you call a feeling of being 'love starved', which makes you need and care too much for the opposite sex. Today, in this modern world, the term 'opposite sex' covers quite a lot of ground and almost anything and everything are now included as an accepted alternative lifestyle, just another example of a changing world.

Your body language is sending off a vibration and it is a language without words. And our inner vibration is actually the truest way to communicate, once you get the hang of it. The most incredible way to communicate with God and this world is by knowing that 'feelings are a language that the universe understands'. Science, also, is a language and is only about 400 years old, as compared to the language of the ancient texts, like the Vedas of India, which are 7,000 years old. Science is also just a story and the newest research is finding that there were advanced civilizations as far back as 13,000 years; and until recently, it was thought to be only five or six thousand years. Well, back to this tale... for the early part of my life, the women could sense that I cared too much and they believed I needed them, which at that time I believed to be true. So, they would just take me for granted. They knew they could have me with a snap of their fingers. It is just basic human nature and how the game of life works. It is not good or bad or even right or wrong, 'it just is'.

It actually is the perfect vehicle for your personal growth, none of the seeming things of life are bad, they are actually there to help us get free of them. Besides, the fact that we are being given the openings to higher levels of understanding, this awakening also gives you insight into the lower physical behaviors of people and also how to master these behaviors. It shows you how to win at the game of life, even on these lower levels, which are kind of meaningless in the long run but better to know than not to know how to master them. So, with this infusion of love and energy my neediness or lack of anything was gone. I felt complete and I could not be happier or more content and I needed nothing or no one. Once again, the language of vibration came into play and the women in my life could sense my feeling of completeness and indifference to them and the tables were turned.

Vibrations are a powerful language without words. It was almost like their egos got involved and they took it personally and unconsciously thought, 'What does he mean he does not need me, I will get his attention' and I would let them do their best. I have actually lived this way for the past twenty-five years and have enjoyed what these wonderful women have given me freely. And of course, I always go the extra mile to make them feel special. I began focusing on my education regarding my own spiritual development and my continued physical training and forgot about the women. As I said, with this new attitude the tables were turned and the women started coming to me. I had finally mastered 'that part of the game of life'.

I would joke the 'Massar of the Game' with an Asian accent, probably not politically correct, but this is a lighthearted tale and humor is the best medicine. This principle of surrender that I had learned regarding woman could also be used in every area of life and you can attract to yourself everything you want effortlessly. The great masters while doing nothing, accomplished everything. It is because we never really do anything, it is universal power flowing through us to create the people, places and things in our life. And to make it even more unbelievable, it does everything with 'zero effort'. In spring, with the flowers just blooming and the trees coming alive, it is all done by Nature automatically and naturally. So too, we can live in the same carefree way. So, the secret is not wasting your time struggling or trying, but to go to source, which is 'your own thoughts and feelings, then see and feel what you want, as if it were already a reality'. This universal intelligence will do the rest. This is the true secret of life and I have used it successfully creating everything I wanted for the past twenty-five years. Also by having lived it I have gained a deep knowing and conviction of its absolute truth and want to share this knowledge with everyone in my unique way.

We are riding the back of a giant and all we need to do is learn how to whisper into its ear, according to Dr. Joe Dispenza. My great friend Tyler would always remind me of his philosophy of life...'Just Passing Through'... and how right he was. This principle applies to this entire physical temporary life we are experiencing in this body. I always felt that certain women were just out of my class and I was to learn that none of them were and that it was all just about my attitude about myself. Think of yourself with respect and in the highest positive ways and you will attract the best of the best. What is that old saying? *Attitude is everything.*

As, it turns out most of the women I have been with were highly formally educated. All had master's degrees and some with extra letters at the end of their names. But, the interesting remark they all made to me was "Peter you just seem to have something that most people don't have and it is a unique understanding of life." I guess some good did come out of this life of self-struggle. That something that I had was just the simple principles of truth, these spiritual principles that I had hungered for and studied for years and eventually I was to become them. They gave me a whole different presence in the world. Spiritual food is just like regular food that we chew, swallow and it becomes part of us. So, it is true with the spiritual food (universal spiritual principles) that we actually become them over time. People may not understand it, but they all feel and will respect the different vibrations emanating from your heart, because of your new state of living that we receive through Grace. I always want to give all the credit to the Grace of God. It is too easy to get a spiritual ego or to forget who you really are and I have worked too hard to get where I am.

A good example was of Barbara coming into my life, who was worldly, wealthy, brilliant intellectually, physically beautiful and truly a sweetheart. Barbara, who had worked as a consultant for Fortune 500 companies around the world, said that I had an ability to communicate better than anyone she had ever met. She would get upset with me when I would mention that I did not have much of a formal education. She would remind me that I have self-educated myself for the past forty-seven years with much higher teachings than those that are taught in the schools of the present-day societies.

Another huge insight from my awakening was that I was to see that what I thought was a wildly, obsessively, overactive sex drive was actually mostly emotional and that I was really craving was Love. Once again, *it is always about Love or the lack of Love.* I was trying to fill that empty hole inside myself and I was looking outward to people, places and things to do it, when the only way to feel complete is to know the Being, God, which dwells in your own heart. Seek the kingdom of God first and all else shall be put upon you. For me, that meant getting to know the God that lives right in my own heart and being established in that love first and then all the stuff of the world just comes automatically without doing anything to make it all happen. I guess there was more truth than I realized in that quote of 'Massar of the Game', as in a sense by knowing God first, you do become the master of your life and this world.

When I began writing these tales I remembered an incident from forty-five years prior, of a night, back in the late sixties, of drinking and drugging. I was with my friend Ritchie, a Golden Gloves boxer and someone who turned out to be quite the seeker. On this particular night, I had drunk a quart and a half of tequila along with taking numerous drugs and I was, to put it mildly, 'almost out on my feet'. Somewhere in the drunken conversation, Ritchie was to mention a book that he was reading about being in a powerful river and just going with the flow.

I literally sobered up for a few moments and had a vision of a black book with a big red circle in the middle and the book was surrounded with golden light. I then proceeded to pass out and collapse on the ground. That vision of this book was forgotten for over forty-five years. Little did I know, but that experience with Ritchie, an unlikely messenger, was my reawakening in this lifetime. It was the awakening of my spiritual journeys from many past lives. I had forgotten about that night until I started writing these tales. I had this inner knowing that the book was *The Tibetan Book of the Dead* and I started looking to find the original copy.

I was not having any luck finding it and at my next visit to the Yoga Center, I mentioned to Martha (a sweetheart of a woman) my difficulty in finding the book that resembled my vision of that night. She said, "Wait a minute" and went to her personal library and came back with a black book with a big red circle in the middle. It was "*The Tibetan Book of the Dead.*" Once again, a cold chill ran up my spine and I wondered, how is all this happening? This might seem like silly coincidence to most, but when coincidence happens hundreds of times, you experience and recognize the connection of all things. I was in good company with *The Tibetan Book of the Dead*, as it was Carl Yung's constant companion.

That seven-year period, I basically did only spiritual practices and had fellowship with other seekers, along with my physical training. It was a nonstop of bizarre experiences over and over. They say when you connect with a true master and a true spiritual path something will happen to you with experiencing stuff you had never experienced before or had ever been capable of doing or knowing. That has been true for me on my own personal journey. I am just writing what happened during this time frame and I leave you to your own perception and belief of what the outer experiences mean. While, all the time knowing that it is all about 'what you experience inside your own self' and not the outer words. Thanks to Krishna Das, I have finally gotten to see that clearly. I have been listening to his Sanskrit chants and realize it is the vibration of repeating these words that reconnects us to our inner self. And, Yes makes us very happy to boot.

I was so excited to be having visions and experiences of things that I had read about from these fascinating, highly evolved beings that had mastered these ancient practices and had taken them to such highly evolved levels of consciousness. I do admit that I have an addiction for danger, excitement and the 'more, more, more syndrome', but this time these addictions actually were a divine gift and benefited me as I used them to dive in deeper and deeper and explore the principles of truth as much as I could. So once again, something that appeared 'seemingly bad', my addictions, turned out to be a blessing in disguise. So, how can you say; something is truly good or bad or even right or wrong? When I see these realizations that go beyond my conscious mind, I always think 'Welcome to Yoga'.

They have a saying about Lynn, Massachusetts (City of Sin), "you never come out the way you went in." Well, I got news for you, once you get involved with a true transformational path (when an awakening happens), that you will never come out the way you went in either. Something happens on your journey, where you go past what the conscious mind can understand and you go into a place of higher intellect and see things in a whole new way, beyond anything you could have fathomed before. Because of our subconscious mind being part of universal mind (God), we have access to unlimited knowledge and are capable of amazing accomplishments. "We are all capable of Great Stuff."

You will begin to live in a world where praise and blame are meaningless and words like 'right or wrong' or 'good or bad', are seen for what they truly are and are just manmade illusions. Man created them to control others, for example, created this misconception of the word 'sin', which actually is an archery term for missing the mark. You become able to 'live and let live' and you let those people who seem to choose to still live in that limited, false world be as they are, while you live in a world that is like Heaven on Earth. The illusion of some being on the spiritual path, while others are not on the path, is truly a falsehood. There is only one road and every human being is on it. We are all just in different locations but all are headed, eventually, to the same destination. I was equally growing on my personal path, when I was involved in ignorance, violence and criminal behavior, as I have been since reading and practicing yoga. It is because of that growth back then, that I reached this way of life that I know today. It is all part of your growth and equally valid and equally necessary. So, who can say or judge, who is spiritual or worldly? Just as all paths lead to the top of the mountain and all the spokes are heading to the wheel's hub, so we all are headed in the same direction to enlightenment.

A priceless gem from the Course in Training is: "If I respect and accept the world as it is, the world will respect and accept me as I am." I love practicing this principle, as I am able to be my eccentric, silly self and live my unconventional life in freedom and independence. I am totally allowed to live freely in this world by giving that gift to others. Can it be explained any simpler? There is a part of your brain (called the limbic) that cannot tell the difference between you and another, so whatever you wish for someone else, your brain will give you that experience 'first' as a gift. I do realize I have repeated some different quotes and the reality is that hearing them just once will do you no good. It takes constant repetition of a statement of truth to finally sink in. So, that's my reason for repeating myself, I am sticking to it. A story told to me by my great friend, Rick Fahey had such a powerful impact on my thinking and acting. It was about the captain at the helm of the merchant ship and the boiler crew doing his bidding down in the belly of the beast. Remember in the old movies, the captain would talk into the tube that ran down to the boiler room and communicate with the crew who were responsible for feeding the coal to the steam engine. The crew would listen intently as the captain said, "more steam" and the crew would 'blindly obey and never question the Captain' and do as they were instructed. What if your subconscious mind acted the same way as the crew when your conscious mind had thoughts? Well, that's exactly how our minds work. Your subconscious mind having 'all power' because of its connection to Universal mind blindly listens and goes to work to create whatever the conscious mind is thinking. The subconscious mind has no opinions, no hidden agendas about anything and exists to fulfill the wishes of the Captain, which is your conscious mind.

Our conscious mind is the supreme ruler in our world. Our subconscious mind is like Aladdin's Genie and lives to obey and serve its master, which in our case, is our conscious mind. "Your wish is my command." God gives us everything that we want and as far as God is concerned, what we think is what we want. So, it is a wise person that checks in on what they are thinking about. *Every thought is creative and there is no such thing as an idle thought.*

The following is a little off Topic, but here we go with some more of the insights or maybe crazy thoughts from this silly Irishman who is writing this book of lighthearted tales. Because 'each of us has all sides of human nature', the seemingly bad traits and also the great, wonderful human qualities, we can think of ourselves at different times as being almost any person out there. We can think of ourselves as any type of individual, attaching our identity of ourselves as that particular type of person. We can identify ourselves with any type of group from the holy rollers, criminal types, bad asses, driven business person, perfect little yogic prissy, helpful teacher, righteous revenge seeker, self-righteous religious individual, etc., etc.

What happens (except for the rare psycho) is if you get involved in one of the violent groups there will be some days where your compassionate and loving side comes into play and you cannot live with your senseless, meaningless, self-centered violent acts. So, what usually happens is the individual will start taking drugs to suppress his feelings and eventually he will self-destruct. He almost always is thrown out of the club or group. I have watched it for over fifty years and had many friends end up like that. I believe I too could have ended up self-destructing like that. Grace had another plan for me. As Jane had mentioned, she has lived a charmed life and it appears I have too. I have witnessed many friends and so-called bad asses have complete emotional meltdowns. No one gets away with anything. The cops may not know about your criminal activities, but in your own heart, your inner self knows. You don't sleep well with carrying that baggage. When you belong to an organization that makes sure that no one testifies against any of its members, many will legally get away with everything and never do a day in jail. I have watched over the years some of these individuals that outwardly appeared to get away with everything and then die young with heart disease and cancer. You kill your own spirit with the violence against others and then the spiritual sickness manifests itself in physical diseases and illnesses.

Anger and hate are worse for your heart than smoking cigarettes, as it constricts the heart's function, even worse than the butts. Our thoughts decide where the energy is directed. Where energy goes, blood flows and where blood flows, oxygen and nutrients go and healing follows. So, if you constrict your energy flow in your heart, it will not only affect your heart but will also affect your brain. It will rob essential nutrients and blood circulation and also constrict your brain function. Don't you think that might be one of the factors to do with Alzheimer's? We can be our own worst enemy because our thinking is the first cause of everything. The anger constricts blood flow and the stress releases hormones that deplete our immune system. Stress also constricts our breathing, which cheats us of our intake of life-giving energy, so living day after day in these states, how could we not get sick? There is only one life force and when you hurt another you are literally hurting your own self. No one gets away with anything and we will experience for ourselves exactly what we do to others and this living planet.

True strength and true power lie within us as love and we can live 'fearlessly' in this world of struggling souls. You will not be afraid or angry with others, who like ourselves, are struggling with the pain of their personal journey. One of the greatest gifts I have received is of living fearlessly, no matter where I am. I know my life is in God's hands and not in the hands of some fool with a gun. The point is that we can kid ourselves into thinking we are just one part of our personality, while in fact, we have many intricate sides. In a conversation with Swami Ishwarananda, a great friend and mentor, I mentioned that I thought I had multi-personalities. He replied: "Or you could look at it another way; that you do what few people do and that is you are not afraid to access all the different aspects of your overall personality. You have gone places most will never venture." He was so kind to me.

The point of this little divergence is that you don't want to deny any part of who you are. And also don't get trapped into thinking you are only one small aspect of the big picture of who you truly are. All these different sides of you are what make you into the 'whole of you'. You will come to laugh at yourself and that is a gift for me, as some of my different sides are pretty preposterous. When a man denies his gentle qualities or tries to suppress them, it makes him weaker. It is all about balance of all sides of our personality. Don't be afraid to be who you truly are and live free. There is no one who can legitimately ever judge you, as God has made you as you are and unconditionally loves you. See only perfection in yourself and the world and that's what you will experience. Something that happens along the way is that words like 'should', 'have to', 'ought to', or 'the right way', will fall from your vocabulary and you will begin to experience true freedom from judgment for the first time. "There is a field out beyond right and wrong, I will meet you there." That was a quote from Rumi.

It is kind of humorous and a little humbling when you realize along the path just how judgmental you really are. We think the problem with everyone else is that they don't know, what we just found out about. I walked around in a daze about most things, for many years and once I saw the truth, I became judgmental and wondered why doesn't everyone see this. In actuality, most of them will see it long before I did.

I had been reading the yogic books for about a year and I had my hands full with all that was going inside me, but the day came that I got the inner prompt to go to an Ashram. I dropped my kids off after our weekend visit; I hit the road for New York. I got there late at night and just slept in the car and went into the ashram in the morning. Some wonderful sweet women greeted me and said the meditation was starting in a few minutes and they took me to this fabulous temple.

You always get more than you expect with a trip to a place, which has done spiritual practices as a way of life for many years. As I sat at the entrance of the magnificent temple as the noon meditation began, I started to sob and eventually ended up on the floor in the fetal position, sobbing like a child. Between my sobbing session with White Feather and now that it was happening again, my Swami friend's words rang true, that this was 'like a purging'. He said: "For all the times you could not love, that sorrow was right in the cells and now it is being expelled. You are truly going through a purging."

I thought I must have been one nasty individual in my past lives to have this much pain stored up. He said: "It is great to see someone have an awakening, but when someone 'like you' has an awakening, now that's really something special." I think he meant it in a good way.

Kay Butler, my great friend, said that someone could have a whole lifetime of just clearing out 'baggage' and I thought since my entering the 12-step program over forty-seven years ago, I have gone through one meltdown after another. Maybe this is my lifetime of cleaning up lifetimes of all the times I was the messenger of pain instead of a bringer of love. I feel compassion for the so-called badass with no conscience, as his day will come and it is not fun when that time comes. There truly is an exact give-and-take in this Universe and every thought and every action will give you the same response back to you, sooner or later. Back in the tale of 'White Feather' I told how I laid on White Feathers healing table, sobbing in the fetal position. I felt the pain of lifetimes of living from the basic instincts of sex, power and control and it was my judgment day. The judgment day, or day of reckoning, is not to do with some outside God judging you, but really a law of Nature, where there is exact balance. What goes up must come down, what goes out from an individual must come back and we will reap what we have sowed. We actually answer to our inner self. No one gets away with anything. We get back what we give out with 'exact mathematical precision'. For every action there is an exact reaction.

I have repeated a couple of statements that can't be repeated enough: There is only 'one' and we are all part of the same one life-giving presence and what we do to another we are really doing to ourselves. This includes this living planet. As we pollute it, who do you think is going to suffer? We are the ones that drink the unhealthy water and breathe the poisoned air. When we dump toxins into the Earth, they seep down to the water table and then we drink them. When we pump toxins into the air, then we breathe them. We dump toxins into the ocean and the fish will intake some of it and then we eat the fish. This is not rocket science, but we continue to do it. When the temperature on Earth was changing, the scientist reported that 'the Earth actually adjusted the planet's temperature, so as to sustain life' as we know it. That is a living and intelligent planet. I often think that Mother Nature gets feed up with us dumping all our garbage and waste into the ocean and responds by spitting it all back at us in the form of a Tsunami.

Well, this book is already a complete success, as in the process of writing this stuff that has been in my head for years, it has given me a clear perspective of the truth. An example of karma is back in my younger days, I had dozens of high-speed chases with all types of law enforcement officers and never was caught for any of them. Years later, after I had really mellowed out and was doing lots of meditation practices and living a quiet life, I went through three years of being pulled over and having my papers run through the computers on a regular basis. I was clean-cut, driving a Volvo, following all the laws and I was being pulled over almost every other week, by every type of cop. I finally, laughed to myself and realized that it was just the law of cause-and-effect catching up with me years later.

The other statement that can't be repeated enough is that the limbic part of the brain can't tell the difference between you or another, or whether what you are thinking is going out or coming in, so we receive first 'whatever we are thinking for another'. If we are wishing them health, happiness and prosperity, we receive that first. If we are wishing them pain and distress, we will receive pain and distress in the form of stress, which will ruin our immune system and leave us vulnerable to diseases. If you want health, happiness and prosperity for yourself, first wish it for everyone else. Try it. It is an amazing gift. 'The Secret' to receiving your deepest desires is to wish the same gifts to others first. Funny, how God set up this game of life. Those pent-up emotions of grief, quilt, anger and hatred, when held inside cause major illnesses and are the cause of most heart problems. The so-called tough guy, who never shows any emotion, usually dies pretty young and miserable. You need to have 'true courage' and be willing to do whatever you have to and get the garbage and hurt feelings out and 'then they will be gone forever'.

My Swami friend had also mentioned that this sobbing is a gift, because if all that negative stuff is left bottled up inside you, it will ruin your physical health. Scientists have found out that it is the source of all cancers. So I received validation regarding these truths from the spiritual teachers and the Western scientists. They have found, through their research, that cancers can be traced back to stress, because stress puts us in the survival mood, which in turn releases all those harmful stress hormones (cortisol). The constant bombardment of these harmful chemicals being released in our bodies eventually results in one form or another of disease. The important thing to remember is that it depletes our immune system and makes us vulnerable to diseases.

When the swami mentioned about all the times I could not love or be kind and instead reacted with violence, it told me once again, 'it always comes back to Love or the lack of Love'. I was so fortunate on that first trip as I got to spend time with many of the swamis (actually spent time with five monks). Maybe they put the word out that this guy should not be roaming around unescorted. Actually, my friend Big Chris thinks that's exactly what they were doing. Looking back, they are so attuned to their environment and may have taken pity on me, as I fell completely apart emotionally. I am sincerely grateful for their kindness and the reassurance, that all of this that had taken place within me was a true blessing. And that nothing was wrong, that this is the process. Basically you feel like you lose yourself, but it is the false self and unreal identity that we cling to. If I can help even one person in the way I have been helped by so many, I truly will be happy.

I did know about a similar cleaning-out process, from past baggage, because of my work in the 12-step program, but it seemed like I had more than my share of baggage. I have been cleaning house for over forty-seven years now; hopefully, I must be near the end. I knew I would live the rest of my life in a way that guaranteed me never having to go through this kind of painful release of bad karma again. Somewhere, in my conversation with my swami friend, I asked him how Yogic paths were not a cult and he replied, Because, a true spiritual path empowers the individual.

The teachings of the meditation master were not to be looking to them for your answers or direction, as all the answers to all your questions are right within you. That is the sign of a true spiritual path, one that 'empowers the individual' and does not try to control the followers. Even in the 12-step program a true sponsor will not run your life, but will show you the tools to find yourself. It is up to the individual what they do with them, as we are all responsible for ourselves. At that time, I had made a dozen trips to the ashram when the meditation master had been there, but I had never even seen her. One night, as I sat at the Yoga Center I was looking at her picture and I thought, *I am surrendering all the way to this process* the following week when I went back to the ashram, I was to meet her. Kind of funny, what a little decision can do. I have talked about how powerful decisions have been in my life, in some of the earlier tales in this book.

I had the most incredible experience when I met the meditation master and this beautiful woman who was joking lightheartedly and talking with everyone. She seemed to disappear before my eyes and all I experienced was a being of pure consciousness. She allowed me to look deep into her eyes and I was overwhelmed with a feeling of peace and safety. Her eyes revealed her true essence, which was of only pure consciousness. Once again, I was in shock with the things that were happening to and for me. I laughed to myself, thinking that where I grew up, we all thought the 'big leagues' was with the power of motorcycles, guns and violence. It was like child's play compared to the power I was witnessing now.

I then heard her say to me without words 'Is there anything else'? And I muttered something like 'I am all set' and I crawled back to my seat completely intoxicated. Well, for me, that was the experience of a lifetime, meeting someone who was living at that level of evolvement. Can I explain the unexplainable? Not today. I experienced the most wonderful meditations and interactions with people from all over the world at this ashram and I was never to be the same again after my visits there. There certainly was no shortage of beautiful women there and they were from all over the world. They do make my journey more enjoyable. I used to joke that when a man finally matures 'like myself'; he has a deeper appreciation for beauty and what is more beautiful than a woman? One day I realized that it was true, that I had a deeper appreciation for beauty and it included sunsets, beaches, women and many other things. Once again the joke was on me and I was the last to know. I returned home from this trip to New York and I was so full of this unexplainable energy that my feet hardly touched the ground. It would be the same with all my trips and I would bring back with me such blessings. It would affect everyone that I would come into contact with, back in Newburyport. The same effect would happen when Chris and Jeff would return from the ashram and they would have a huge effect of the local inhabitants.

Chris and Jeff, two friends that I shared the lessons of the correspondence course with, made many trips to the ashram and yoga centers and were having the same kind of revelations. We shared some of the best times of lighthearted fellowship that I have ever known. We truly had great times sharing this journey together. It was pretty humorous, as the three of us really stuck out like sore thumbs at the ashram. We were a little rough around the edges, compared to the perfect yogic types. There was not much the three of us had not done during our lives and our body language still showed it. I will always cherish the time that I spent there and it has left an indelible mark on my heart. These trips were also a part of that 'seven-year cycle' and a lot has changed from those days. You will have to bear with me as I use the word 'yoga' to cover all my experiences. I hopefully someday will be able to explain all these incredible experiences and have the right words to go with them, but for now, I would be hard pressed to explain the miraculous accurately.

An example of the kind of personal energy that you will acquire from these yogic practices is shown in this next little story. Big Chris and I had finished doing a long meditation along the river and we were just sitting quietly. A state policeman passed by and then turned and came back and came up to us. He could sense something and was trying to get an idea of what we were up to. I calmly told him we were just enjoying the river and his agitation increased. He went back to his patrol car and called for backup. Now picture two people sitting quietly after meditation, no outward apparent threat, no guns, weapons, or drugs, yet he could feel the energy that we had raised up in meditation. Backup with the police dogs showed up and now they are tearing my car apart and Chris and I could barely keep from laughing uncontrollably. Our laughing would have sent the cops right over the edge. People fear what they don't understand. This cop knew something was going on, but it was nothing he recognized. Yeah, it was fearlessness, peace and contentment. The cops did their whole intimidating routine on us, to no avail; neither Chris nor myself could care in the least what they did. Even a beating or shooting us would have been meaningless for us. We could not be shaken from the fearless state of being that our meditations had brought us to. They finally gave up and left in a huff. Chris and I were still sitting in the same spot, doing the same thing we had done the whole time and we just turned our attention back to the river. The state cop was actually a really good cop, with great intuition. The problem was that he did not recognize the state we were in and it was completely foreign to him. So, his reactive mind kicked in and thought there was some kind of threat.

Some of the other things that started happening to me after returning home from these trips involved my friend Tyler, a semi-pro football player, college basketball star and custom motorcycle builder. It is interesting that if you live in this neck of the woods, even if you are not a football fan, eventually you will become a Patriot's fan, as they are such a remarkable group that just pulls miracles out of their hats, game after game and year after year. Years back, I had my mind totally on my studies and training and was not aware of what was happening in football. As a result, I had a clear mind and I started predicting which years the Patriots would win the super bowl and the years that they would not even make it to Super Bowl. For years, I was having this 'knowing' of what the Patriots would do in that particular year, sometimes before the season would start. Tyler is someone that is very observant and one year he had invited me over to a Super Bowl party and I said I was going to stay home. Tyler replied there is plenty of food and you can sit with my big-breasted girlfriend. I replied: "I will be right over." Tyler had told me that on a number of occasions when they would be out at a bar, he would hear her say, "Do you think my breasts are too big?" Tyler would turn and she would have her top pulled up. So yeah, I will be right over. She truly, was a pleasure to even just look at. There is one thing that the people of this world can agree on and that is, 'Everyone loves Breasts'.

During the game Tyler would say, "Hey Guru, what is going to happen next?" and I would turn from my deeply philosophical conversation with his girlfriend and tell him what was going to happen next in the game and exactly what I had said would come to pass. This went on all through the game and as it was nearing the end it appeared that the Patriots were going to lose this one. I stopped from my engaging intellectual conversation with his girlfriend and said, "Don't worry the Patriots are just making you sweat, but they are going to win with a field goal." And that is exactly what happened. Then I promptly returned to important matters of discussing worldly topics with his well-endowed girlfriend. These last few Super Bowls I watched with Barbara and would tell her before the game whether they would win or not. She has been amazed that I have predicted every game accurately for the past ten years. The game with the Seahawks, I had a knowing they were going to win and it appeared that I was going to be wrong for the first and only time. I thought, it will be the first time 'My Knowings' have been wrong and it did not seem right. Well, as you all know, they pulled another miracle play from their specialty playbook and won the game.

So, my predictions have been 100% right, but I know if I try to use them to gamble they won't work, so don't ask. One of Jane Nock's dogs is named Gronk; that tells you how the people around here feel about the Patriots. Erik's dog was named Harley; that show the love of these great machines that are responsible for a whole way of life. This book being all about the mind, focus, attention and putting your heart, mind and soul into whatever you are doing could have just been told by telling the Patriot's story. The Patriots are the best example of these principles you could ever find; such an amazing group of people. Since then, I have really become interested in the game again and I have lost my insight into the outcomes, due to having a personal interest in the game, again. How could anyone watch this team and not become a fan.

As I write this story I am getting to see what a big part Tyler has played in this story and how he is disguised as this big, carefree jock and is actually someone that is very enlightened. One day, as we were watching a game from this second-floor building, all the birds were going wild out in the trees, which were about the same height as our view. Tyler said: "Hey Guru, would you ask your little friends to quiet down so we can hear the game." I had this 'knowing' that something was going to happen. So, I stood up and raised my arms straight out and slowly lowered them and when my arms reached the bottom every bird stopped chirping.

Now, I had thought God had worked through me to open Tyler's mind, but when Tyler jumped up and yelled, "I knew you were going to do that," I realized, that it was '*his belief in me*' that had drawn that experience right through me. So, Tyler is the real Master of the Game. I was working, with Tyler at this family plant in Amesbury and we were filling jars from a huge kettle that contained liquids that could fill any number of jars from a hundred to four hundred jars, with no way to tell how much would come from a batch. I had just come back from a trip to the New York ashram and I was flying with the energy from the trip. I had covered the worktable with caps for the jars and I was asked what I was doing and I replied: "I think this is the amount of caps we're going to need for this batch," and everyone laughed. As we reached the end of the batch and there were only three caps left on the table, Tyler looked at me with a very serious look and said: "You are going to be damn close." Well, they scraped out the last of the batch and poured it into a jar and I put the last cap that was on the table on the last jar and everyone just got quiet. There was no logical answer for how this could happen and it could never have been guessed by the conscious mind. But our subconscious mind, being a part of the universal mind, which is connected to everything, can do anything.

As of late, when my time with Barbara had ended, Tyler has been reminding me of the powerful positive thoughts that I had shared with him years ago. He is a very supportive friend at this time of change for me. Years ago, when I would share the yogic teachings with him I never was sure whether he was just humoring me or he was taking it all in. Today, his life reflects someone that has really adopted these teachings as a philosophy to live by, as he will always remind me that we are 'Just Passing Through'.

I told him I was impressed with how he had used these teachings and he responded: "I had a good teacher and that was you." You never know who is listening.

The other day, I was sharing one of the stories with Tyler and he said: "Pete, you are using some big words in these stories" and we both laughed. Tyler will live a long life, as he has the ability to laugh at himself or to make light when things don't go his way. There is no better feeling than sharing these teachings, as they can make the difference between someone being stuck and miserable and someone truly having the freedom to live.

So, I was to continue having wonderful meditations and contemplations all along the river and Market Square with the energy from this lineage of meditation masters that was now flowing unimpeded through me. Along the way, I was to see just how conditioned and programed I was from family, society, schools and groups, which had little or no real knowledge of how to think or live or the truth of life.

It truly was my time to live the life I wanted. The place to start is by asking yourself, *What do you think life is all about? What do you think is truly important and lasting?* This is a great place to start. Take some time and go for a walk on the Newburyport boardwalk, as it is one great place to do this type of contemplation and to just sit quietly. And, just let it come to you and then contemplate your insights. The river will pull you right into a meditative mood. It is one of the strongest forces of Nature that I have found and it is right there at the boardwalk.

A remarkable technique for knowing what you truly want is in the following: When you have a question that needs to be answered, sit quiet and ask yourself *What do you want to do in regards to this situation?* And don't answer it quickly with your head, which is your programed, conditioned mind of right and wrong, should and have to's, *but let it come from inside you.* If it does not come the first try, just try later or the next day and keep doing it and one day a voice from deep inside you will speak to you. You will have guidance directly from God and a tool to live the rest of your life with. I have used this technique more than thirty-five years and it has never failed me. Another way to answer questions is laid out so clearly by Deepak Chopra and is as follows: Sit quietly and ask yourself, *What happens when I think of going in a direction regarding something?* You will get a feeling, sometimes very subtle feeling, but either a gentle calming sense or a nervous agitated feeling. It is the Universe directing you which way to go. If you get a calm feeling it is the cosmic computer giving you the OK to proceed. If you get a nervous uncomfortable feeling, it is your inner self, saying this is a 'no no'. It can take some practice to get the hang of it, but it is so well worth it. Also, it does take time to learn the difference between your head and feelings lying to you and your intuition about things, which is divinely inspired. Just some practice and you will have very powerful tools for making decisions in your life.

The first time I used this tool was when my girlfriend at the time got pregnant and I had to decide what part I was going to play in this situation. I sat each day and used the above process and nothing was coming and then after days of sitting and waiting, I sat again and on that day, I once again said: *What do I want to do in regards to this situation?* And from deep inside me separate from my mind and body came a voice saying: *I want to have this baby more than anything else in the world.* Wow, that is not what Mister Irresponsible expected, but the birth of my son Benjamin really was a huge turning point in my life. This was another transformational time in my life and changed everything in regard to how I live. This is one of the inner treasures (powerful tools) that have made my life in this world so enjoyable and an infallible method to get proper direction regarding which way to proceed with your life.

This is my little tale of Shakti Burn.
Peter James Ford
The Cider Hill House

I spent countless hours doing my practices in my little slice of Heaven. That was a rare female wooden carved Buddha that Barbara had rescued and restored from an antique store in Maine. It is now sitting in her meditation room in Los Angeles, California. All my love goes to Barbara Parton.

When all is said and done, 'It is always about Love'

Another way this could be said is that it is always and only about Love or the lack of it. Truth, Love, Being and Consciousness are words that are all interchangeable and all have the same meaning.

If you take a close look at what is happening in the world today, you will see people either being loving and creating a wonderful world for themselves and those around them, or you will see people living from a place of fear and coming from basic instincts. The latter are coming from the lower chakras, the lower energy sources in the body. These lower levels are from the place that our sex, power, struggle to survive and control drives come from or our appetites for sex, possessions, dominance over others, control and the more, more, more syndrome. Faith, from the Yoga Center, affectionately would call the men coming from these lower chakras as the 'knuckle draggers' (the caveman). Who are trying to bang everything on two legs and taking by force whatever they want. It makes me think of the term 'common man' as most live by these basic instincts.

The four basics of the animal side of human beings are feeding, fighting, fleeing and making babies (F-word). It was humorous when Deepak Chopra mentioned that is how he heard it explained using the 'F word' in medical school. When through grace our hearts open, we begin to live in a higher place of Love, Compassion, Non-Judgment, Kindness, Generosity, Contentment, and begin to Freely Give. We live in a place of not needing anything from anyone, which frees us from desire, jealousy and envy of others or their possessions. This unconditional love of God awakened in your heart makes you feel like the wealthiest person in the world. So, naturally you begin to think in terms of giving to others, instead of taking from them to fill all your imaginary needs. This Love is the source of true freedom and happiness and actually is the only real and lasting happiness in this world. All that we truly have is the sharing of this love with other people and everything else is just a passing temporary illusion. Chronis, the Greek God of Time, whose number was *seven*, said that anything temporary was not truly whole. We may not be able to feed all the hungry of the world or create world peace, but in our little world we can affect those in our immediate environment and play our part right here and now. Not many of us are meant to affect huge numbers of people so be content with being there for even just one person. That is your part. If you are not there for them, who will be? I thought if someone in the 12-step program only helped one person and that it turned out that one person was my son or daughter, would I not think his life was worthwhile. The answer from me would be a big yes.

When I walk the beach with my granddaughter Shayla and watch her exchanging unconditional love with the people on the beach and with their dogs and the deep love she has for the animals, I know this is the only true reality in this universe. All else is just a temporary passing show. So for me, after all is said and done, 'It is always about Love'. I also love to remind myself that it is a new day, a new beginning, that life goes on and to focus straight ahead with your dreams. When people that you love leave you, just be grateful for the time that you got to share with them and know that was then and this is now. Look to the new day and straight ahead with living in this present moment. Today, the expression 'just keep trucking' has new meaning.

An insight, that I had one day, while I was dwelling on some negative stuff was the thought, *Don't I have anything better than this to have on my mind*? Actually, anything would have been better and I just shifted my thinking to something uplifting and immediately felt great. Another huge realization for me has been seeing over and over again how this life always comes back to just one story. I have shared this one story all through this book, in one-way or another. I suppose, it will have to be something that each person experiences for himself or herself. I don't feel that I can accurately put into words what has happened for me. It turns out that it is not that easy to explain in words, 'the unexplainable'. How could I put into words the feeling of being intoxicated with God's love? Just know 'all roads' eventually lead back to God. All roads lead back to your own heart. The destination is your own heart. I will leave the explanations to the much more knowledgeable writers and wise men to tell the tale of this worldly/heavenly experience and I will just happily read their words. I have seen that what people really want is to simply be known and accepted for who they are. People just want to live their life in peace. This book has been my vehicle for this acknowledgement and acceptance of who I have truly become. God has worked miracles in the life of this old soul and this life is the culmination of many, many years of spiritual practices.

I love being Mr. Nobody as it is so freeing and takes all the man-made, self-made pressure off of me. I can just wander this world being a carefree man fully present in the moment, enjoying Nature, the company of a beautiful woman and riding in the mountains. Sounds like a pretty great existence. There are much more qualified people to explain these secrets than me. For me, it is similar to being back in the sixties and trying to explain your LSD trips. Words just could not do it justice. Speaking of LSD use, I came across this article on Steve Jobs, who was the CEO of Apple and learned the same lesson from his life: It is all about the mind. Steve was one of the most successful entrepreneurs and also dropped out of college and had used LSD. What changed his life was his 'Seven'-month trip to India. 'I know another seven', actually I have had a dozen more sevens in the last week. I also forgot about a whole section of sevens to do with all the Terrorist Attacks. Sevens all through the attacks in these past years, it actually was kind of spooky, almost like a pattern.

Well, the point of this little section about Steve Jobs, besides another 'seven' is that he did not go the usual route that society says to go to be successful. He dropped out of college and spent his time focusing on his goal. His mantra was *'Focus and Simplicity'*. I have heard that all through my readings, especially Ram's teachings. At Steve's funeral he had someone give out copies of *Autobiography of a Yogi*, by Yogananda, one of my favorite books. A formal education does not necessarily give you an understanding about the principles of life or even guarantee that you will be successful in the material world. It is because the subconscious mind of every individual knows more than any college library and can be accessed by any one of us.

After reading Vince Lombardi's mission statement, which was all about positive thinking straight ahead, seeing and thinking only what you want. I smiled, and thought how successfully he had used these principles of focusing the mind, repetition and only thinking about what you want and disregarding everything else. Actually, some of the most successful people who got their recognition in athletics or other areas of life where actually so proficient at using these ancient universal principles. When you look at guys like Tom Brady, John Cena or Vince Lombardi who are such successful athletes and realize they are some of the best examples of the spiritual practices of controlling and focusing a disciplined mind. I am just continually validated and overjoyed with who I have shared these same principles on my journey. Oh Yeah, I can't look anywhere without finding another 'seven' and Vince was no exception, as he was a member of the famed "Seven Blocks of Granite," a name given to the sturdy offensive football line at Fordham University. I am starting to think I should have named the "Tale of the Sevens" the "Curse of the Sevens," as my daughter Rachel had suggested, as they just won't stop coming. Really, this is the last two, but when I remembered the Seventh ocean wave is believed to be the largest wave and called the seven-wave maxim theory and a whole science in and of itself, I just had to add it and the other one is the 'Seventh Wave Laboratories' representing a unique alternative to drug development.

So, really the conclusion of this book is about three subjects and they are 'After all is said and done, it is always about Love'. The second is that 'It is about controlling and learning to use the awesome power of the mind'. Knowing that all the successful people in this life went to the same source of all knowledge and power and they accessed this knowledge 'through their own subconscious mind'. It does take a little practice and repetition, but it has nothing to do with a high IQ. Actually, some of the people who are so intellectually smart will have a harder time with these teaching. So maybe that was what was meant by 'the Meek shall inherit the world'.

You can visualize multiple desires, but focusing all your attention on just one goal is the most effective. Put your whole mind, heart and soul into heading straight ahead to your goal and you will be unstoppable. See and feel your desire with all your heart, soul and mind and fill it with enthusiastic emotion and you will wake up one morning and it will be in your life. I am feeling and seeing my copy of *Mysticism in Newburyport* sitting on the table at Barnes and Noble. Your continued focus on what you truly desire and the consistent repetition of the practices needed for that particular task will bring you to your goal. Only think about what you want and feel it like it is already a reality in your life and continually focus on this goal and you will have your desire. I have found that focusing on one goal at a time really is the most effective.

Right now, all my attention and focus is on completing my first book and 'let's see what happens'. Also keeping things simple, because that helps keep your focus from being distracted by all the other stuff going on. And the third, on a lighter note, is all the sevens and seven sequences that show up all through this life. And, if anyone knows what the real secret of the sevens is, please write me and tell me. I am more of a gatherer of the sevens and honestly I am not sure what it means, other than knowing that life is made up of seven-year cycles. So, my telling of my experience of seeing the same story played over and over again before my very eyes can only allude to the following experience. Just know, that this worldly life is like the movie "Groundhog Day" and it will go on and on until we master it, which really is becoming the master of our own mind. 'It is all about the mind'.

As, I have mentioned before in this book, I had the insight of seeing what the word Universe meant, Uni meaning one and Verse meaning story or text. So the one word for this Entire Universe means One Story. And that story is The Play of Consciousness, also known as The Play of God. It is kind of humorous because this was one of my Big Insights and last week as I watched Wayne Dyer in one of his last presentations, he talked of how the word Universe meant One Song. I laughed as I thought that God does not let me get any ego strokes. I think that is my friend Sandi's and my granddaughter Shayla's purpose in my life. They make sure to keep my ego down to the right size. God is much too wise to let anything go to my head, as my own accomplishment.

When I was twenty-five years old, I had been sober for six years. I had done another moral inventory with Father Kevin of the Arch Street Chapel in Boston. We took a lunch break and as I sat in a restaurant experiencing such peace, the woman sitting at the next table looked up and said: "You have such a peaceful presence and you have an amazing look about you." Looking back, what I was experiencing was being fully present in the moment. What a coincidence, that is the name of Ram D. R. Butler's course, "Living in the Truth of the Present Moment," and the purpose of his course is to show you how to do that. This existence of ours is truly about becoming fully established in the present moment. In Buddhism, it is called Mindfulness in the Moment. In Yogic terms it is called Fully Present in the Moment. Thoreau called it The Bloom of the Moment. To be established in the present moment causes your life to be a series of unending miracles.

The other priceless gift I have received is the ability to be guided and to live my life from my intuition (my sixth sense), which is direct and infallible guidance from God. I do not make decisions or judgments by the outer appearances or what the limited five senses tell me, but I just listen to that inner voice deep within my own heart. It did take years of trial and error to know the difference between my conscious fearful mind and my ego or what was my divine guidance coming intuitively from my inner prompts. God wants to give me a win in every situation and all I need to do is listen to the gentle inner voice. I have developed the ability to sit quietly and experience direct conscious communion with God, wherever I am. What a gift! No worries, anyone will eventually get the hang of it and then you will live in a whole new world of light, love, beauty and abundance. I feel it is the promise land and I visualize living in a land of beauty, light, love, abundance and prosperity.

As I walked the beach the other day, it was cloudy with a light rain and with almost no one on the beach. I saw this woman standing quietly looking out at the ocean. As I passed, she turned and smiled. We began talking about how most people do not even see the beauty of this moment. Her name was Carly and she was an absolutely beautiful twenty-two-year-old and was so awakened and tuned in to Nature. She was such a gift that morning, as I was thinking I would never meet anyone as compatible as Barbara was for me in my life again. God was just showing me how everything is available in every moment for the person who is fully present in the truth of this moment. She was physically beautiful and had the same love of Nature and being connected with God as I do. I did realize my relationships with women are changing a little, as the part that I might play for them is different, but even better. She was truly awakened and feeling like she was on the wrong planet, being so sensitive and appreciative of all God has given her. I shared books and information about the stuff that has helped me so much and encouraged her to find likeminded people. She said: "I feel like I just did with meeting you." I shared about this book that you are reading and that Newburyport is really the heart of the story and Carly responded: "I was born in Newburyport." I would love to be twenty-five again and carry her off into the sunset, but I find myself playing a different role at this point in my life. It is more of sharing this great information about life and being supportive to people.

One day I laughed, as some people were looking to me for some direction and I thought: *Really? I am the voice of reason?* God has such a funny sense of humor. Most of the people in my life today have no idea where I have come from and it will be interesting to watch their reactions and perceptions of me now that I have shared so openly. Once again, let the chips fall where they may. I have mentioned previously about Dauchsy Meditations and it is just such an important piece of information to know and it is as follows: The time when you are almost falling asleep and the time when you first wake up are the two times you have the most power to influence your mind. If you think about what you want as you are falling asleep, your subconscious mind will use that for the entire night's sleep, playing over and over like a song you can't get out of your head. This repetition is impressing your thoughts 'hopefully what you really want' into your subconscious mind and will eventually manifest in your life. The other time is first thing in the morning, as you can set your day on the right track. Most of the day, you are on auto pilot and the things you have gotten clear about and have put your intention on, first thing in the morning, will cause your mind to go in that direction all day long, 'automatically', without you even thinking about it. How powerful is this stuff?

Dr. Joe Dispenza takes two hours every morning and creates his day, right there and then. Similarly, as Ram D. R. Butler has explained, that he no longer likes to leave the results of anything, up to chance, he sees how it will end before he begins. Seeing is the creative process and we literally see and feel things into existence. Your life will be what you believe it to be. If you don't believe me, just take a look at the person who thinks life is hard and you see he never really gets anywhere. Isn't his life just like that? Now you look at that happy, optimistic person who thinks this is a great life with great people and is his life not a life of everything going his way? Just take a few slow breaths and look around, that is all these Masters did was to see what was right in front of us and only disguised by our having our eyes closed.

Something else that is priceless to me, and yes, it is another of Ram's treasured wisdom, and that is that the breath and mind are connected and we can literally control and quiet our minds by controlling our breathing. Long slow breaths in through the nose and long slow breaths out though the mouth. God gave us free will and free will is the choice about what we think next. Think uplifting, optimistic, kind, loving thoughts and live in a wonderful world. Think negative, gossipy, judgmental, depressing thoughts and live in a terrible world. Consistent negative thinking will cause the stress and will make you old and ruin your health. That does not sound too appealing, but we automatically do it without thinking until we wake up again in this life. Both a great life and a terrible life are fully available right now. What do you truly want? And yes, you will have to go against what most of society will tell you is true and it will feel foreign at first, but you can do it. Anyone can do it, because of the gift from God of freewill, which means 'the choice about what we think next'. Think happy, positive uplifting thought and that is all it takes to have a great life. Throw in a little gratitude and you will be golden.

All we have is a very short time in this body. I want to feel good and be at peace and fully enjoy all the gifts of God, Nature and the company of a beautiful woman in this present moment. From these teachings, I truly love being healthy, happy, and successful in everything I do, living in abundance and enjoying all of God's gifts to me and us. Come join me, on an endless holiday and let the world play its silly games of jealousy, judgment, greed and self-centeredness. I love this quote of Ram: "If I accept and respect the world, as it is, the world will in turn, will accept and respect me as I am." Another one is, "When I refuse to play the game of this world (by having no opinions), I am out of the game and free." Just let the world be as it is, it just is what it is.

My friend, Sandi and Shayla have really hit it off and they enjoy ganging up on me, and keeping me in my place. I am grateful for both of them, because better people than I have gotten off track with their egos. I have worked way too hard to get where I am today, so thank you God for my continuous ego deflation (usually with Sandi's and Shayla's help). They both seem to love to keep a man's ego down to right size. I love them both with my whole heart. Shayla and I watched a Harry Potter movie and Hermione was a very supportive friend to Harry. I said to Shayla that she could be supportive to Grandpa in the same way that Hermione is to Harry and she said: "That's not going to happen."

We both laughed. We share a funny, wonderful relationship, where she can be truly herself without any fear of an adult correcting her. I love watching her be able to just be herself with me, without any fear. I realized that my being a male figure that she can freely say how she thinks and feels, without any fear of reprisal is a priceless gift for her personal development that I can give her. I hope it increases her ability to freely say how she feels and not to be suppressing anything. Being a grandpa is such fun, as I will keep her safe when I am with her, but I allow her to express herself freely. I am just there for her.

Shayla and Grandpa

Have you ever seen a great athlete who may not be a very articulate speaker or may not be well educated, that when he gives all the credit to God for his great performance, you will notice people give a smirk or laugh behind his back? Little do they know how right on he is and his humility is such a divine gift. It was God's energy/grace flowing through him and he intuitively knew it. That's a wise man. He knows how to stay out of God's way and let the grace flow through him by his being humble.

The incredible thing in this life is that a human being can actually find him or herself and know who they truly are. The eternal vigilance part comes into play, with the fact that they can once again lose themselves. That is why I give all the credit to God, including anything worthwhile that comes from this book. The ancient seers and seekers discovered the secrets of this world long ago by turning inward, and they have left the information for us to rediscover in our own time and in our own way. On a public television special about how the scientists built a listening radar/device dish to be able to hear out into the universe, the scientists did hear something and it was a vibration and they said it sounded like OM. It only cost six billion dollars to build and I thought the little yogis have known this for thousands of years and probably would have told them the answer for a handful of rice placed in their begging bowl. When the scientists look for the end of the Universe, the act of their looking creates more Universe, so there will never be no end to this vast Universe. As I have said, it is hard to put my experiences into words, but you can experience this for yourself through any one of the many spiritual paths that are available, if you have an inclination to know. These practices can give you the priceless gift of: *Your mind will become like a lamp set in a windless place.*

The incredible secret to healing is so simple. The body is throwing off huge numbers of cells in every moment and creating huge numbers of new cells, in every moment. This intelligence behind Nature is in every cell of your body and takes its orders from what your conscious mind repeats. So, if you continue to think that you are in perfect health and feel how you would feel if you were in perfect health, right now, and be grateful for it, you will come to be in perfect health. Our own thoughts are the only cause of everything in our life and this Universal Consciousness is like the Genie in Aladdin's lamp: "Your wish is my command." The key for me was when I realized and knew in my heart that the intelligence behind Nature was also in every cell of my body and responded to my thoughts and feelings. If you want to talk about 'real power', that statement is a good place to start.

We try so hard to understand the workings of the world, when what is important is understanding the power that can create or do anything at any time in the world. Knowledge of God is Power, and Self-Knowledge (the God within) is the ultimate power and the key to health, happiness and prosperity. The purpose of this book is also to maybe make you think about different things that just go unnoticed. One interesting thing was of certain dates in time, like Ram Butler being born on the 4th of July. My father a good Irishman, passing on St. Patty's day. Teddy Roosevelt's wife and mother died on Valentine's Day and I was born on Pearl Harbor day, the Seventh.

We have been so fortunate to have Teddy Roosevelt, as with his insight to preserve Nature and make it available through our National parks. Teddy spent time in seclusion in North Dakota and said that he would never have become president if it were not for his time in solitude in Nature. Really, another great person that got his strength from Nature and Solitude. It seems all the ones that have done great achievements in the world have spent time doing some type of spiritual practices. Steve Jobs, of Apple fame, his mantra was of Simplicity and Focus. Steve took an unconventional route to find himself, but look at the way he has affected the lives of so many of us.

It seems that everyone that has been successful has made it through learning how to connect with him or herself first. Churchill, Einstein, Henry Ford are just a few that have made statements of how they used the power of thought to achieve incredible accomplishments. I mentioned in a past story about on 7-7-17 I was to have a medical procedure, a biopsy. Once again, it has come back a clean bill of health, after the doctors did everything to scare me. The last three years, I had all the physical tests they give a man when he gets into his sixties. And there have been times my mind got the better of me thinking I could not live the lifestyle I love. Growing old gracefully is something I might consider when I am in my nineties, *maybe*. I choose to think I am young and full of life and in perfect health. Well, the great news is that after all these tests and procedures, I have a clean bill of health and the doctors said that if everyone were in the health you are in, we would be out of business. Thank you God and now I can fully have my mind on acting like I am a healthy twenty-five-year-old, all-American male again.

I suppose, in lots of ways, this book is just trying to interest people into finding their 'own discoveries' about this wonderful life and planet. The inner treasures are just waiting to be recognized and aroused. Our subconscious mind is truly like the Genie in the bottle. We have a sleeping, all-powerful giant right within us just waiting to do our bidding. Just control your thoughts and think only about what you want, and ignore any discouraging or disparaging thoughts and see where it takes you. Environment is huge. I needed to get the negative people out of my life and replace with supportive, uplifting people. You need a safe environment where you can let your guard down and allow yourself to feel what is in your heart somewhere it is safe to breathe. I think of that priceless gem from Louise Hay: "It is safe to breathe, it is safe to live." I spent most of my life with contracted breath, the way you unconsciously breathe when in a danger zone or a coalmine.

That knowledge was such a gift to have, to be aware to only have safe people in your life and to breathe fully. There is something called 'Email Apnea' were you start breathing constricted because you are writing an email to do with a stressful communication. It should not surprise us, as that is what we do in any stressful situation. It is one of the first things a good trainer will teach you in fight training and that is to stay calm and how to breathe fully and normally, as someone is throwing punches at you. The Navy Seal training pushes them beyond all limits and teaches them how to keep a cool head in the worst situation. Pretty amazing people make it through that training. The guys that swim out of Boston Harbor, out to Graves's lighthouse way out in the ocean, do it by controlling their breath.

Something that has worked wonders in keeping me free and not allowing myself to be trapped is that I have lived my life 'doing what I what to be doing'. The way out of any situation is doing what you want to be doing. People say that you can't live like that. Actually you can and you can live really well. I learned this when I was ten years sober and it is one of the most powerful and freeing tools that I have used for more than thirty-five years. I may be different than most, but I need to know I am living the life I want to be living and not being a robot who is just doing what his peers want. Asking yourself *what do I want to be doing?* This will bring rigorous honesty to yourself. It is how we get out of God's way, by not pretending to do the right thing and being good little doobies. Don't make any waves and just stay in line, like a good little soldier that blindly follows orders. Sorry, that's not for me. I let no one or anything stand in the way of my freedom and independence.

True courage is when you can be honest with yourself and be true to yourself about the life you want. I am so glad I took the leap of faith and found true freedom. It is another paradox that when you give yourself unconditionally to God you actually become 'Independent' and free to live the live of your choosing. Remember that at the end of your life there will be no one there to judge you, except your own inner self. And if you have had the courage to be honest with yourself about who you are and how you want to live, you will be happy and there will be no judgment.

God wants us to take our rightful place in this life and we do it by knowing that we are a part of God and 'God's powers are our powers'. We hopefully will use them in a positive creative way. I just keep thinking how important it is that we realize that we all are like little Gods creating our lives in every moment with our thoughts, feelings and attitude. Some creating great lives and some creating terrible lives. I know I have created both. It truly is about returning home and the destination is our own heart. Marianne Williamson has it so right when she wrote her book "Return to Love." Marianne found the same secret, as I have found and is that the destination is your own heart and your own love. Yes, she is another dark-haired beauty, which takes my breath away. Well, one thing that has come out of this book is that it is pretty obvious I have a deep affection for the dark-haired women. I do believe it is from past lives and it has to do with the Native American women and the Asian women. As I write this, something else has just been answered: My fascination with the women is that I have always seen the Goddess manifesting as the woman, even as a child. I will say once again, there is something magical about writing stuff out. It actually is not magic; it is that you are in direct conscious communion with God.

Another of the clear knowing in my life today is that life goes in roughly seven-year cycles and the creation of this book started in the seven-year cycle just prior to meeting Barbara, my karmic partner of the last seven years. This book was almost completed seven years ago and upon meeting Barbara, it went on the shelf. Barbara's loving presence in this world and in my life was similar to a whirlwind courtship and a seven-year nonstop honeymoon and don't get me wrong, I am not complaining. Our lives and experiences together were so full and fast paced; it was more of a case of me hanging on for the ride and not having much time to focus on completing this book. Huge pieces of karma were being burned off very rapidly and everything happened exactly as it was meant to.

Louise Hay tells in her book of herself being someone who was not formally educated or very worldly and when she met her husband to be, a wealthy, educated, worldly Englishman he taught her a lot about life. She said she was extremely grateful for the time together with him.

My experience with Barb was very similar, as she was beautiful, worldly, brilliant and a well-educated woman. Barbara was knowledgeable about wealth, spiritual practices and had lots of life experiences. Just as Louise was grateful for her time with the Englishman, I too am sincerely grateful for my time with Barbara. We lived a wonderful life together of unconditional love and of truly having a home and a full life together. This was aside from the main purpose, which was fulfilling some karmic needs. When the time was over, God provided the least painful way for it to end. I am not saying that the ending of our time together was without pain and sadness, because like the end of any relationship it had its adjustments; but God really made it as quick and painless as possible. We parted on great terms and remain best friends. Barbara will always have a special place in my heart. Barbara will always have a piece of my heart, as only a few other exceptional women do.

Our Thunder Mountain Customs
I truly love my bikes.

The hardest part of this book to write was the dedication, as in the writing of these tales, I was to see how miraculously I have been taken care of by a loving God who worked through so many, many people and how many wonderful, true friends I have in my life. I could have dedicated this book to my children, who are such an amazing gift to me. I could have dedicated it to my parents or the 12-step program. I could have dedicated it to the Meditation Master whose energy enlivened the teachings and this book. Easily could have dedicated this book to Ram and Kay and the course as the service and information that they have shared has transformed my life. The list just goes on and on and the realization of how blessed I have been. My sponsor was right when he said, that The Man Upstairs worked overtime taking care of me.

As I look over this book, I see some little mistakes in grammar, but it does not matter. It is all about the Intent of these writings and the 'Intent' is to share my experience, strength, and hope. It is to share my enthusiasm for life and my gratitude for having been so blessed with so many great friends and loved ones. I know, I know, I have turned into the guy I always have made fun of. God has such a sense of humor and, once again, the joke is on me.

I add a special thanks to Krishna Das. Ram had mentioned that sometimes he would listen to Krishna Das' chants as he wrote the lesson for the correspondence course. I began listening to these chants as I was working on this book and an amazing thing was happening as I would get so clear and it seemed to really influence the flow of my writings, so big thanks to Krishna Das. I also watched another video of Krishna Das and he talked about his reason for chanting was to save his ass and his life, not to become something or someone. He said: *"It was his way of cleaning out the dark corners of his heart and clearing out the shadows."* Once again I was in awe knowing I am following in the footsteps of people I really respect. The last seven months of writing out these tales has been my way of cleaning out all the dark and heavy corners of my heart and getting rid of all the shadows of my past. As, Krishna Das has found his practice (chanting) in this lifetime, I too, have found my way and that is in my writings. These types of practices are incredible transformational and priceless gifts.

Ms. Barbara

Barbara had driven my 120 Race Road Glide coming back from a visit with
the brothers in Laconia, NH. No one could keep up with her.

So this is my simple book of tales, which is a complete success already, with me seeing how blessed I am and how I have lived the perfect life for my personal evolution. This life and this book truly could have been called a labor of love. This book of tales is basically of this simple man trying to add his experience, strength and hope to a greater good and possibly help touch even one heart. My story is everyone's story. It is a story of human nature and a story of our divine nature. I hope you have enjoyed these tales.

As, I have said earlier in the stories that I had tore these stories up three times. I never wanted to be this honest. I never wanted all (well most) of my secrets on public record. I never wanted to open myself up like this. I never wanted all my pain and struggle to be out there for anyone to know. In the end, when you get an inner prompt you blindly follow it. God calls and you answer. By surrendering to God you will know true happiness and peace for the first time. For some reason God wants my story told. It is interesting to observe how in the last seven months of writing this book, my understanding of life and myself has already changed again.

These stories have already starting touching hearts, even before finished publication. Sandi, who I mention often, as she is someone I really care for. She had mentioned how truly happy she was for me getting my book published. She said: "She is usually so wrapped up in herself that she rarely thinks of anyone else, but that she was experiencing something new. It was true joy and happiness for me." The book is already a complete success as it has already touched one heart and that is Sandi's heart. Sandi had mentioned that a change in her personal life caused her to feel like a failure. On our journey in this life we will have a lot of losses and 'seeming' failures. In the eyes of the world we may even appear as failures. We are made in the image and likeness of God. In God's eyes we are perfect. Which view do you choose? I choose God's perspective. I encourage anyone that is in a dark place in his or her lives to hang in there. Know, that if at this time in your life you are alone in your secret pain and personal struggles that many before you have come out of even worse times. They have gone on to know true happiness and a fulfilling life. There will come a day where someone very unusual comes into your life and will reach deep inside you to that secret, special, private place within your own heart and touch you like you have never been touched before. Your life will be changed forever and all your fears and worries will be ancient history.

There is always hope.
God always answers despair.

"Dust in the Wind, in my case, Crazy Dust in the Wind"

PETER'S PERSONAL METHOD FOR MANIFESTING

Something very important to know is that the two most important times to influence your mind is when you first awake in the morning and also just as you are falling asleep. As the Yogis get up at three or four o'clock in the morning when the Earth is asleep and in a different mode, so to, our brain is in a different quieter mode and easier to access the different deeper levels of consciousness.

You can set your mind and day with the intentions you release first thing in the morning. Most of the day you are operating on automatic, so setting your intentions first thing in the morning, sets your subconscious into action and will automatically make the decisions corresponding to your morning intentions, without you even thinking about them. Instead of repeating the same old, same old, your subconscious will be finding opportunities and directing you in positive ways to bring you to your desires.

Then, at night, as you are falling asleep your brain and mind are once again in the most receptive mood. Whatever you are thinking about just as you are dozing into sleep will reverberate into your subconscious mind for the entire night of your sleep. Your subconscious will use your last thoughts for the next eight hours to create your desires. Actually, this is the best time to create, as your brain is in the best mode for manifesting, because your body, that has become your unconscious mind is asleep. Through repetition our body becomes the mind. It is just as the boxer who will respond without even thinking from all the repetition he has done in his training. From all the training the boxer's unconscious mind is now in his body and the body will react like it has a mind of it's own.

Some scientists are doing great work showing the different phases of the brain (Beta-Alpha-Theta-Delta) showing people how there are certain times that are the best to access deeper levels of meditation and consciousness. Science is just validating what these ancient masters called the inner technology of meditation, consciousness and the science of breath. The Scientists discoveries affirm in a little different wording the same ancient truths and principles. Today there is a growing community of scientists combining western science and eastern wisdom and running incredible healing workshops. Sometimes it takes a year or two but people are being cured of incurable diseases after being written off by doctors. I have mentioned these pioneers earlier in these tales.

First, you will want to relax your body and mind. You can use any number of simple breathing exercises to accomplish this. Your mind and breath are directly connected. It is easier to access your subconscious mind when you are relaxed. One way is to slowly breathe in deeply and then to breathe out slowly and completely. This will relax your mind and then you can do a simple guided body relaxing meditation, if needed. There are numerous ones on YouTube. So, you need to start by gaining control of your mind and body, as there is no proficiency in anything without first establishing harmony.

Then, we have to get really clear and specific knowing it is something *"that our heart truly desires."*

I love cigarette-racing boats and Las Vegas Showgirls, but do I *"really want to have one of them for real?"* The answer is not really, both sound like a lot of work. They are fun to think about but my heart does not truly desire them. So, I am honest with myself and don't waste my time on anything other than something *"I want with my whole mind, heart and soul."* Remember, to create something it needs to be what *your heart truly desires.* You will know the difference, as once in a while it gets really clear and your heart feels like it is going to burst with enthusiasm, that's how you know. Listen to your heart. Your own heart holds all the answers for you.

It is about specificity (being specific). It is about clarity (being clear). It is about making it very personal. Additionally, putting yourself in a relaxed state makes it easier for the Universe to create your dreams. Also, which is huge, is saying: "I am." Saying I am directs Universal consciousness through you into whatever you believe. When I was first with Barbara, I was watching the DVD "The Secret" and it talked about imagining something that was so big that you would have no doubt that it was created by these principles. I thought, I have a compatible woman, what could be greater than that? I thought, ok, let's have some fun. I thought, here I am on the biggest, baddest, sixties style chopper with a massive racing engine and the color was green with a touch of gold. Despite the fact, that the color green was taboo in the outlaw biker world, I loved that light green filled with gold color. I visualized every day and one day I walked into Seacoast Harley-Davidson in Hampton, NH and on the floor was a Thunder Mountain Custom Cycle out of Colorado. It had just arrived and was exactly like I pictured, right down to the exact colors in the paint job. That is the power of making your dream very personal, very specific, seeing it very clearly in your mind as already a reality and filling your vision with enthusiastic emotion and gratitude. Do this and you will have your desire.

So, after you get clear about what you want, then it has to be something that you believe is possible. If you have doubt you can, through repetition, bring yourself to believe it is true through repetition of its existence. Day after Day of repeating your desire, visualizing it, feeling it as it is already real (Ex: I am a published author), then one day you will get up and say "Yes, I am a published Author." You will awake one day to know it as true in your heart. *You will have created the belief* and then it is only a matter of time and it will manifest physically. It will be *compelled* to manifest in the physical world.

You will be creating *emotional, sensory rich thoughts and visualizations* of what it feels like, looks like and even smells like to already have what you want. The more emotion you put into it, the more real it becomes. It will become clearer and it will become more and more powerful every time you see and feel your dream. (From Dauchsey's thirty-day challenge on YouTube).

As an example, I have written a book about to be published and I found a book the same size and put a picture of the cover of my book with the title on it over the other book's cover. Every morning I sit and hold the book and look at the cover of my book, I feel the texture of the vinyl front and back cover of the book. I turn the book over and see my Shayla on the back cover dressed as 'Belle' from *Beauty and the Beast*. I hold the book's back cover with Shayla's picture to my heart and just feel unconditional love. I open it and feel the parchment of the pages as I turn them. I smell the paper and ink. I feel the pages between my fingers. I look at the book and hold it and know it is all completed and is in bookstores around the world. I create emotional sensory rich thoughts and visualizations of my completed book.

How would it feel if my deepest desire were already real? What that does is bring up an emotional response of a "Big Yes!" I would feel wonderful and that is the fuel I power my visualization with.

Now that your desire is real, how does it affect your life? Well, for me this book is going to put me into a whole new world of accomplishment, being welcomed into an even more highly evolved environment and it changes everything in my life for the better. This book has already changed me and *I am* entering a whole new world.

How will this desire (my book) affect the people in my life? I will receive a new appreciation for who I truly am. People will never look at me the same. I often will hear, I had no idea who you were. I am receiving appreciation for acknowledging all the great people and giving this special part of the world (Newburyport area) the recognition it deserves. When I realize that feeling of appreciation, it creates a wonderful powerful emotion that is making my dream even more real. Every day it grows more real in my heart of hearts.

Take a deep breath and breathe out as you release your desire, your breath will increase the intensity and make it even more powerful. Once again, I see the correlation with the boxing, martial arts, swimming and spiritual practices. It is about controlling your breathing, controlling your focus and knowing how to use your mind. All these practices are necessary to be good in any walk of life. It always comes back to one story of life and existence.

The key is to really desire it, to really get clear that you want it and are willing to go all the way believing in your dream, to really visualize and feel it as already real and believe it is true now. After weeks of doing this practice regarding my book, I believe in my heart, mind and soul it is a reality. I went all the way believing it is true and real. It is now created on the subtle level and must manifest in the physical world. *I am a successful published Author.* It is the continual mental repetition of what you truly desire and doing it consistently everyday and seeing it as real that will compel it to manifest in the physical world. There are unfailing laws in this Universe and when we learn how to align ourselves, miracles happen.

Believing it is possible and true is the big thing. Repetition of your desire (even if you doubt it is possible) will eventually cause the effect of "Came to Believe." All day long say, "Yes, my dream is true!" Everything already exists in the quantum field of all possibilities just waiting for us to call it into existence. A child dreams about what they want at Christmas with no thoughts of cost or how it could be possible. The child only thinks about what they want. That is what you want to do as well. You want to develop the faith of a child. Trusting in this power greater than us. As my granddaughter, Shayla, said to me with a little smirk: "I am a kid I never worry about money." As Aladdin's Genie said: "Your Wish is my Command." The Genie is our subconscious mind that is a part of Universal mind (God) and is able, willing and "Eager" to fulfill all our dreams. The Universe does everything with zero effort, so why are we struggling and worrying?

Naturally, we do our part and for me that is getting very still early in the morning and just before sleep seeing, feeling, believing, smelling, touching and holding my completed, published, new book. I see all the wonderful pictures of my life, page after page and I am filled with emotional gratitude for the gift of this incredible life I have lived. This emotion fuels my visualization and the emotion makes it even more real. This visualization and emotion brings my book to life. The Universe will do the rest and take care of all details. How powerful is this truth that God is able, willing and even eager to make my desire (my book) a reality. God is in every atom, ever cell of every living thing, in every particle of consciousness. God is connected and a part of everything and God is eager to make my book a reality. Wow! OK, I have done my part, so let's see what God has in mind for my little creation called *Mysticism in Newburyport. I am* standing in Barnes and Noble's bookstore holding a copy of my book in my hands, as a beautiful young woman says: "That looks like an interesting read." "Yes, I think you will enjoy it and the author is equally interesting." lol. Remember this is book of *lighthearted* tales. So let's see what happens.

Some people learn information and then selfishly keep it to themselves, believing there is only so much to go around. The Universe is endlessly bountiful and if everyone fulfilled all his or her desires it could not possibly deplete the Universe. Endlessly bountiful means Endlessly bountiful.

In the 12-step program it said: "Receive freely and Give freely." I choose that philosophy and I freely would give any knowledge that I have received through grace to anyone that was sincerely looking. Yes, my only enemy today is my ego and it is constantly looking for something to latch onto and identify itself. I freely give all information to all, as the more people whose life improves; the better the world will be for all of us. So giving freely to others is a win-win for everyone. We live by the philosophy that we have come to believe and my way of living is just giving away everything freely as that is how I received in the 12-step program. God hates a void, so if I give all, God will fill me back up.

These are the personal treasures that I cherish and use and have used for twenty-five years with absolute success. So, if you are reading this book that will mean once again, this process was a complete success.

Thanks to All
I wish everyone Health, Happiness and Prosperity
God is riding on our breath

HELPFUL BOOKS

The following information is about the different sources that were so helpful to me on my journey of re-awakening. It will also include information about the correspondence course by D. R. Butler (Ram) on the principles of truth that was so incredibly transforming for me, and also helpful DVDs, in addition of other books.

The Course of Training, which I live my life by, is called "Living in the Truth of the Present Moment" by D. R. Butler (Ram). Everything that you could possibly need to live a completely full life in this world or to understand the ancient truths, regarding the Spiritual path, are all covered in this miraculous course of training. Ram's course is directly connected with two ancient unbroken lineages that go back five or six thousand years in written form and possibly longer. In these lineages, these ancient Masters focused every breath and every moment on spiritual development and practice. Can you imagine the enormous amount of energy that flows from 'thousands of years' of practicing the same principles? And because of Ram's course, this energy and these teachings are available to you, right now? The energy, which flows through his writings, came from these ancient seers and Masters who had devoted their lives to the development of these inner powers. These are ancient sciences that hold unimaginable power. These lineages go back to the times when Egypt, India, and Tibet were at the height of their spiritual evolution, even including records and teachings of Christ that are recorded in their ancient libraries. Their records show a very, very interesting story of the one called Christ.

The Tibetan Book of the Dead not only played a huge part for me, but it was also Carl Jung's daily read. I was in good company. *Man and His Symbols*, by Carl Jung, was another fascinating read and also revealed how simple and obvious man's behaviors have been though the eons. I was in good company, as the book called *Autobiography of a Yogi*, by Yogananda, was also a favorite of Steve Jobs, of Apple fame. *The Tibetan Book of the Living and Dying*, by S. Rinpoche, was another great book. *Key to Yourself*, by Venice Bloodworth, a priceless gem of a book, which has been a daily read for me for twenty-five years. *Seven Spiritual Laws*, by Deepak Chopra, another easy to understand guide for the laws of being. Any and all of Wayne Dyer's writings are such a gift to humanity, as are all of Deepak's writings. Joseph Campbell's books and quotes are priceless gems.

Heal Your Life (DVD), by Louise Hay, owner of Hay House International Publishing and just an absolute sweetheart of a woman, is another 'priceless treasure'. One huge gift from Louise was how she associated living and breathing together, in her first pamphlet, and how it is safe to live and 'it is safe to breathe'. My breathing was always in a contracted state, I was always in the fight-or-flight mode and the words "it is safe to breathe" rang home for me. It took me most of my life to relax and to know how to live, and to finally know it was safe to breathe. I was not in a war zone in my head anymore, and I realized how contracted my breath had been all my life. The study of breath is a whole science, in itself. The book by Yogi Ramacharaka called *The Science of Breath*, was another priceless gem, as was his book *Hatha Yoga*. It is so interesting that simple techniques that provide perfect health are completely overlooked, by most of society.

Meditation, a practical survival kit for the 90's, by Allen Holmquist, is a guided meditation DVD that is incredibly informing and so relaxing. Allen talks of what I would call a love affair between people and the plants and trees. Allen explains how we breathe out carbon dioxide that the plants take in to live, and the plants and trees breathe out oxygen, giving us life. We truly are one with the earth.

Awakening Shakti, by Sally Kempton - I had the privilege of meeting and listening to Sally share her wisdom years ago in upper state New York. Sally profoundly touched my heart and I have never forgotten the love that radiated from this sweet woman. She was utterly amazing. Sally's workshops will change your life forever and I am sincerely grateful for her love and the spiritual energy she has shared with the world.

The Yoga Vasistha, considered possibly the most complete book on the mind, was an incredible read. *Jnaneshwari's Gita*, Swami Kripananda's commentary was priceless. Any of Swami Muktananda or Chidvilasananda's books are uplifting beyond what your conscious mind could believe possible. Swami Anantananda's book *What's on my Mind*; he was so kind to sign my copy and I am grateful for our conversations. Any, of the vast yogic teachings are full of transformational treasures, worth more than gold or silver. The principles of truth not only give you complete happiness, they also show you how to easily create gold, silver and all the worldly stuff, if that is what your heart truly desires. My experiences at the various ashrams I visited cannot be put into words. My experiences were beyond anything I knew to exist in this world. I had lived by my five physical senses, which are so limited and when the inner psychic senses are awakened, all else is revealed. The interesting part is when you start living this way of life from these ancient teachings, which at first seem so unbelievable, it quickly becomes the only way you would live your life, ever again. There is no going back to a life of unconscious living.

As I am doing the last read through with this book, my great friend Kay Butler has sent me a copy of the novel *Shantaram*, by Gregory David Roberts. This novel has already grabbed me in just the first few pages. What an incredible life story this man has lived and written about.

These are some of the books and places that transformed my life from a boring, struggling, depressing and average existence to a life of continuous experience of 'Heaven on Earth' here and now and also for eternity. My life has become a continuous cycle of daily miracles, by just having *the right attitude and correct understanding of life and myself.* Once that re-awakening to your true self happens, you will never think of yourself as anything but the most blessed person in this life; Knowing with every fiber of your body that you are in God's hands and that you have always been and you always will be completely taken care of.

We all will have a certain individual, mentor, writer or path that just reaches in and touches our hearts, opens our minds, and gives us the direction and support to follow the spiritual path to completion. In the end, we realize that everything leads back to 'one source' that all paths lead to the same place. The destination is 'our own heart' and we will finally know it, for the first time, as the resting place of God. You will know for the first time that there is nowhere else to look, nowhere else to go, but to just dwell within your own heart, the abode of God.

You could say that God and Heaven live right here, right now, in your own heart and mind. You will know that you are finally home. You will live fearless, even in the worst of times. There is no power greater than the Love of God. There is a feeling of complete contentment and peace that comes from finding your true self and you will know that every moment from now on, is equal to every other moment.

And so, you 'just simply live' and you live in complete gratitude, with peace of mind and a sense of well-being. And you will be thankful for just another cherished moment of life, for just another breath of life. Just our being here calls for a celebration. You will lose your fear of death, as you will know that there is no such thing as death, and that your true self is eternal. You will know that no one ever goes anywhere when this body falls away, as the physical and subtle worlds (subtle world is the world of your mind, emotions, spirit and your eternal essence) are present and intertwined, right here and right now. I feel the presence of loved ones like my Father, Big Ben and Dave Nock, as strong as I did when they were still in their bodies. There is a way of being so much more aware and in tune with the world we live in by using these simple ancient practices. You will know that the state of joy that you are in now will be the same state of joy you experience when you leave this body. You will know your life is completely in God's hands and with complete abandonment you will live every moment to the fullest. There is nowhere to go, there is nothing to acquire, there is no one to be concerned about, and so, you will just simply live.

People say that time is speeding up and they are right. The scientists say the pulse of the Earth has speeded up. So time is flying, but 'you can actually slow time down', by the simple practice of being fully present in this moment. When you start being conscious of this present moment, time will slow down and the time you have left in this body will seem a lot longer than if you are unconsciously living life.

I love the statement of the Zen master: "Before enlightenment you lug water and chop wood and after enlightenment you lug water and chop wood." That always brings a smile to my face. It is such a humbling statement and it tells you that you are no better or higher than anyone else. You will still have your human side with all its faults and flaws, but you will know that is not who you truly are. You are a manifestation of and a part of God. God is manifesting as you in this very moment. You will just know for yourself that you are complete, within your own self.

I hope my words from my personal journey may be helpful to you on your search for yourself and the God of your understanding. When I read that the purpose of the book of the 12-step program was to help you find a God of your understanding, I thought, how divinely inspired was that book. Always know that those who sincerely reach out shall always receive, and if you ask for help and guidance, it will come to you. And if you are in tough times know in your heart that *God always answers despair*. I am living truth of that last statement as I have experienced the depths of personal despair and I am still here to talk about it. It is darkest before the dawn, *but the new day always comes*.

If you are still breathing, no matter how bad your situation appears, you are still in the ballgame and miracles can happen at any moment. It is hard to accept sometimes that there is a valid reason for everything that happens in your life. The darkest periods of my life have always been followed by incredible periods of joy, abundance and recognition of being at a newer and even higher level of personal development. The painful changes in my personal life this last year were the cause of this level of honesty and openness that you will find in this book. It has given me a level of abandonment to this process we all go through in this temporary incarnation. Everything has a purpose and nothing is wasted. All pain and struggle is all for your personal development and this book would not exist if I had not experienced the same tough road in my life, as does every other human being. Truly, my story is everyone's story. Countless others could have written this story or an even better story, but for some reason God has worked through me to create this little contribution for the rare individual that could identify with a life like mine.

When I was twenty-five years old, my depression and my feeling of being hopelessly trapped were so unbearable that I put one of my guns to my head, but I could not pull the trigger. I have had a number of friends that did pull the trigger. Like them, I would have missed out on so much. God's way of healing us is letting us forget our pain and we once again start to live. The answer for me to live a great life was learning how to think correctly and that is what changed my life so drastically. I will be eternally grateful for the universal principles of truth that I first found in the 12-step program and then in Eastern Philosophy. Hang in there! It is so well worth it. For what is on the other side of the pain will be truly amazing and you will think to yourself, *Of course, this is so obvious, why did I not see it before?* This is just how the game of life was designed. Initially we might not like it, but we don't have to fight it, it just is how it was set up for people to grow.

"We can fight it or we can go with, as if we were in the current of a powerful river." That was Ritchie's statement to me in 1968. We just need to survive the tough times. The trick is to relax, control your breathing and pace yourself, during the hard times, just like Navy Seal training and also how a boxer trains. They will train you never to lose your cool, even when being hit and how to control your breathing in even the toughest, most stressful of times. The same training is all through the martial arts. It always comes back to one story: If you lose your cool in the ring, you will be exhausted quickly and weakened. So it is in life. You always want to stay in control of your emotions, mind and breathing, otherwise they will drain all your physical strength and leave your immune system vulnerable to diseases. Always remember that your mind and breath are directly connected and you can control your mind with simple breathing techniques. How great is that? Also, what does not kill us makes us stronger. So either way we win. You either will be dead and at peace or you will be stronger in a new, even better place.

Barbara has said to me a number of times that I think in a very different way than most people do. She said: "I am not saying it is wrong, I just never heard someone speak like you do, it is similar to someone speaking in a foreign language or kind of like in parables." I do think in my own little way that I have become a storyteller. I always loved relating the wild interactions with the people that I have met on my journey. Some of the outlaw bikers were like colorful, modern day pirates.

Well, the real reason for writing these tales was from having a constant and continuous inner painful prompt and a need to get these things out of me and onto paper. Then to share them and then to let it all go, as if I have no past right up to this moment. This book is giving me a clean slate for my entire past life and has opened a new door to a whole higher level of existence. Thank You God. I really was not one that wanted to share or reveal himself in this way, but when I get that inner prompt, (which I believe is direct guidance from God),

'I answer it.'
No matter how painful the past,
Always look to the Future.
There is always Hope.
Dream Big and Live Well.
The Author Peter James Ford

ABOUT THE AUTHOR

The author was born an Irish Catholic, down in Lynn, Massachusetts on December 7, 1950. The Author never did well in this religion and even got physically sick in church, on a regular basis. They were happy to see him go. After seven years in Catholic schools, the Author went into the Public School system and never opened another book again, for twenty-five years. In the sixties, they started something called social promoting and this program was basically, if a student showed up a certain number of days for school, he was passed on to the next grade.

So basically, the Author has a 7th-grade formal education and he has been self-taught through years of reading Eastern Philosophy and from his own personal life experiences. He has spent the past twenty-five years reading, studying and practicing meditation for four or five hours a day and physically training four or five hours a day, also. This routine has been his life for the past twenty-five years. There was a seven-year period that the author lived in Newburyport, Mass. and the book was based on his meditative and spiritual experiences, in this magical, little town.

After a number of years of this practicing, the author experiences an outflowing of insights and experiences, which he wrote down as this book. He felt as if he was just a witness to this information that seemed to be flowing from an unknown source. It truly seemed like a mystery writer was behind this unfolding process. So, in this book are contained his experiences, insights and realizations. The author actually tore up these writings three or four times and it is a miracle for them to be in print. The Author spoke of something happening inside him, with the realization of just how temporary this life is, after experiencing the passing of a number of significant people in his life. A new level of freedom from caring or worrying came to him, as the author knew that one day he also would leave his body. This knowing helped establish the Author with being fully present in this moment and to make the best of every precious moment left in his life.

At the time of this writing he is living for the summer in the quaint town of York Harbor, Maine and thinking about his next book. Some of those stories will be: The Rise of the Warrior/Ego Society, The Metamorphism of the 12-step program, The Science of Numerology, Religion versus Spirituality (the age old question) and Shifting Sands. His story is just one of the many individual stories of people re-awakening in this lifetime and who are growing in enlightenment. He hopes that this lighthearted book of tales, if nothing else, brings a smile to your face.

This picture is from one of the Author's many trips to the White Mountains with the perfect bikes to climb the hills.

The Author's Road Glide was powered with a 120 Race engine, with 140 Horsepower and 140 Torque and he would ride a wheelie, while smoking the back wheel.

Once again, a Special Thanks to the techs, for putting this beast together and to all his friends at Seacoast Harley Davidson in Hampton, NH.